IMAGES
of America

McMinnville

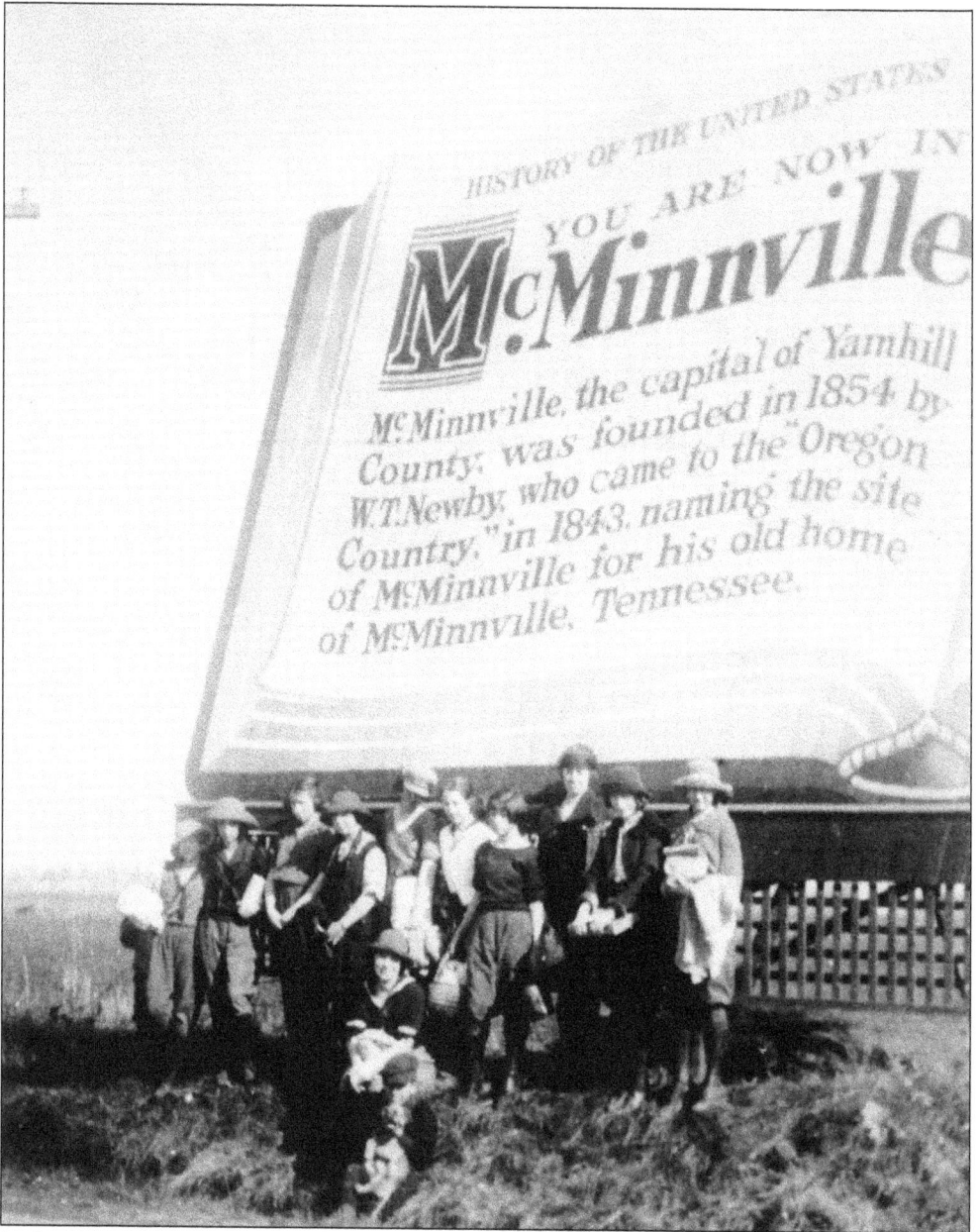

In the 1920s, a new billboard was placed along Highway 99W on the north entrance to McMinnville near the current location of Cascade Steel. A group of women poses in front of this sign, which reads, in part, "You are now in McMinnville. McMinnville, the capital of Yamhill County, was founded in 1854 by W.T. Newby." (WO.)

ON THE COVER: On March 22, 1952, some employees of Vinton and Larsen have gathered to celebrate the repainting of a vintage car at Goodwill Used Cars, which was a Pontiac Motor Division merchandising program. The car is a 1915 Buick Touring Car that had originally belonged to the Talbot family. Pictured are, from left to right, Worley Burnett, Don Mitchell, Larry Ritland, Ervin Kroll, and Lloyd Ollis. (LA.)

IMAGES
of America

McMinnville

Christy Van Heukelem, Tom Fuller,
and the *News-Register*

ARCADIA
PUBLISHING

Published by Arcadia Publishing
Charleston, South Carolina

Library of Congress Control Number: 2011939020

For all general information, please contact Arcadia Publishing:
Telephone 843-853-2070
Fax 843-853-0044
E-mail sales@arcadiapublishing.com
For customer service and orders:
Toll-Free 1-888-313-2665

Visit us on the Internet at www.arcadiapublishing.com

This book is dedicated to the residents of McMinnville.

CONTENTS

ACKNOWLEDGMENTS

The authors would like to acknowledge the assistance of the following individuals and organizations without whom this project would not have been possible: Jeb Bladine and Karl Klooster of the *News-Register*; Jean Caspers and Susan Barnes Whyte of Linfield; Brian Richardson (whose history of businesses in McMinnville was an invaluable resource); Wes Thompson and Patrick Quinn of McMinnville Water and Light; Kris Gullo at the Downtown Association; Patti Webb from the Yamhill Enrichment Society; Mike Colvin of Chuck Colvin Auto Center; Allan Larsen of Larsen Motors; Steve and Scott Macy of Macy & Son Funeral Home; Eric McMullen at the McMinnville Fire Department; Tami Spears and the Wortman family; Kris Olsen at McMinnville High School; Chris Jenkins at the Community Center; Sandra Van Bergen at St. James Church; Belinda Garrettson at First Presbyterian Church; the First Baptist Church; DeArmond Bockes at the Elks Club; Waldo Farnham of Farnham Electric; Mike Full and Nancy Law from the McMinnville Police Department; Glenn Shipman with the Yamhill County Sheriff's Office & Masonic Hall; Janmarie Delschneider; Maxine Marsolini (who edited the manuscript); Lindy Batdorf; Susan Scovell McGregor; Matt and Marilyn Worrix; Richard Ulrich; the City of McMinnville; and the staff at the McMinnville Public Library. We would also like to thank our families for their support – you're the best!

IMAGE CREDITS

CC	McMinnville Community Center
CI	City of McMinnville
CO	Mike Colvin
DA	Downtown Association
FA	Farnham Electric
FD	McMinnville Fire Department
KB	Key Bank
LA	Larsen Motors
LI	Linfield College
MA	Macy & Son Funeral Home
MS	Masonic Hall
NR	*News-Register*
SL	Oregon State Library
UL	Richard Ulrich
WA	McMinnville Water and Light
WO	Wortman family

INTRODUCTION

William T. Newby was born March 23, 1820, in McMinnville, Tennessee. He was orphaned at a young age and later moved to Missouri, where he married. When he was in his early 20s, Newby found himself lured west by the prospect of founding a new commonwealth on the Pacific coast and by an environment abundantly suited for cultivation. He and his wife, Sarah, joined the first wagon train across the Oregon Trail and arrived in Oregon City in 1843. The following year, they relocated to Yam Hill (Yamhill) County. He set down roots on the site that would form the nucleus of the city of McMinnville. In 1850, Newby received title to the land he had claimed through the Donation Land Act. The Newbys had eight children, but not all survived to adulthood. Newby died suddenly in 1884, two years after McMinnville incorporated. His dream of forming a vibrant city lives on.

McMinnville has grown into the most populous city in Yamhill County and is home to Oregon Mutual Insurance and the Evergreen Aviation Museum. The museum houses the iconic *Spruce Goose* (Hughes H-4 Hercules Flying Boat), one of the largest aircraft ever constructed. One of the most charming aspects of the city is the quaint downtown core along Third Street. Many of the original buildings remain today—a testament to the enduring vision of William T. Newby, who desired a town in the upper Willamette Valley. His participation and ongoing influence over the birth and evolution of McMinnville are threaded throughout this narrative.

Some milestones in McMinnville's history are listed below:

1882   McMinnville incorporates as a city with a mayor and city council
1889   *Telephone-Register* newspaper created
1899   Long distance telephone connects Newberg and McMinnville
1905   McMinnville Chamber of Commerce forms
1910   Lincoln High School is built
1920   McMinnville's population reaches 2,767
1922   McMinnville College becomes Linfield College
1923   West Side Pacific Highway opens
1928   Numbered streets are reversed
1938   Highway 99W bypass is built
1945   Property for airport is purchased
1952   Adams and Baker Streets become one-way
1960   Evergreen Helicopters incorporates
1970   McMinnville's population exceeds 10,000

One

BEGINNINGS

In 1844, William T. Newby arrived at Yam Hill County, at the point of present-day McMinnville. At that time, only six residents lived nearby. He claimed 640 acres between Cozine Creek and the Yamhill River, before the time that land rights in Oregon were deeded by law. Newby built a cabin near the site of today's public library, in the area of Baker and Third Streets, and began working the land. Other settlers migrated and, like Newby, began cultivating crops. In 1846, Dr. James McBride, arriving on the Oregon Trail, became one of the area's first physicians. By 1847, churches began to appear in McMinnville. Aaron Payne, minister of the Christian Church, was recruited by town residents to also serve as schoolteacher. For $5 per student, Payne taught both children and adults, from 6 to 60.

By 1853, the village had a gristmill and, shortly after, a blacksmithy and a store, clustered near Newby's cabin. Sebastian Cabot Adams Jr. and McBride joined with Newby to create a school that later became McMinnville (Linfield) College. These new amenities drew more settlers. Newby donated land for their use in exchange for building structures on the land. He also donated five acres to define, lay out, and establish an official town plat. Adams, a teacher and surveyor, plotted the streets. Newby named the fledgling settlement McMinnville, after his home in Tennessee.

Although the town had a name, it was not yet the center of Yamhill County. About 1856, nearby Lafayette had a population of 800, a post office, church, school, and 10 shops. McMinnville had only 27 residents. By 1870, the population trend reversed, and McMinnville's population doubled that in Lafayette.

Getting to and from the new town of McMinnville was difficult, especially when transporting heavy freight or grain on wagons along the old Native American trail. In those days, it was not uncommon for a wagon to become mired axle-deep in mud. Efforts to improve the road to Portland were mixed, and often summer's work was washed away by winter's floods. Boats were navigable up the Willamette and Yamhill Rivers, but only to the rapids at Lafayette, except during floods. Steamships passing through these waters bore the names *Hoosier, Washington, Multnomah,* and *Canemah.* It was not until the railroad arrived in 1872 that the town could easily connect to the outside world.

By 1869, community leaders had convinced some important businesses to relocate from Lafayette to McMinnville; in 1872, this included a predecessor to the *News-Register.* And, by appealing to Joe Gaston, Newby was instrumental in channeling the railroad through McMinnville, which, naturally, had a profound impact on town growth.

In 1876, McMinnville became incorporated as a town, with designation as a city following in 1882. In 1887, an effort to move the county seat from Lafayette to McMinnville was initiated. Supporters of the move contacted area settlers, excluding those in Lafayette, for balloting. By the time the citizens of Lafayette discovered the plot, it was too late. The vote had already taken place, and McMinnville was the clear choice. The new courthouse was completed in 1888 at a cost of $70,000.

William T. Newby, born in McMinnville, Tennessee, was one of the first settlers to arrive in what would become McMinnville. He spent his life pursuing a vision to develop a Pacific town, and his efforts gave birth to the city of McMinnville. (Author's collection.)

A mill, completed in 1853, was McMinnville's first commercial building and was key in assuring the success and prosperity of the early community. The mill changed hands several times. The rebuilt Star Mill (pictured) burned to the ground in the 1920s. (CI.)

The most expensive part of the mill, the millstone, was manufactured by an Oregon City millwright, ferried across the Willamette River by boat, and loaded on a sled pulled by oxen to McMinnville. The heavy stone is still on display behind the current library near the site of the mill. The mill was called the Kinney Mill after 1860, when Robert Kinney purchased it. He sold it in 1868, but the name stuck. (CI.)

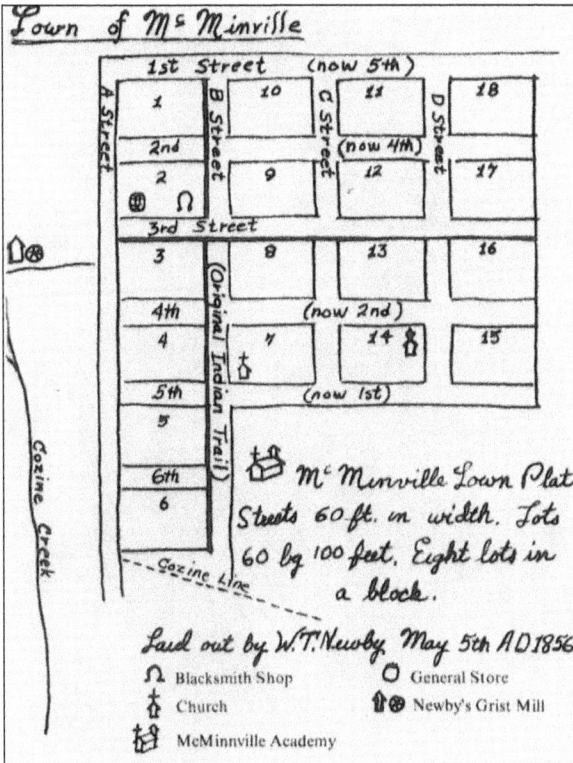

Town of McMinville

1st Street (now 5th)

A Street

B Street

1   10   11   18

2nd   (now 4th)

C Street

D Street

2   9   12   17

3rd Street

3   8   13   16

(Original Indian Trail)

4th   (now 2nd)

4   7   14   15

5th   (now 1st)

5

6th   McMinville Town Plat

6   Streets 60 ft. in width. Lots 60 by 100 feet. Eight lots in a block.

Cozine Line

Cozine Creek

Laid out by W.T. Newby, May 5th AD 1856

♒ Blacksmith Shop   O General Store
⛪ Church   🏠⊕ Newby's Grist Mill
🏛 McMinnville Academy

In 1856, Newby laid out this city plat on five acres he donated to the town, naming it McMinnville, after the Tennessee town of his birth. The town was centered on an old Native American trail, now called Baker Street. (CI.)

Unconscious and nearly dead after a difficult journey along the Oregon Trail, Sebastian Cabot Adams Jr. arrived in Oregon in 1850. He recuperated and moved to the new settlement, where he taught school and surveyed land. Adams married Martha McBride, helped found McMinnville (Linfield) College, and went on to publish the well-known *Chronological Chart of Ancient, Modern, and Biblical History*. (SL.)

Martha McBride was the daughter of Mahala and James McBride. She crossed the plains to Oregon in 1846 and married Sebastian Cabot Adams Jr. on February 6, 1851, in Yamhill County. Martha gave birth to a son, John Quincy Adams, in 1859, but he died only six months later on April 1, 1860. In 1881, he was reinterred in Salem, Oregon. Martha died in 1882. (SL.)

Adams and his wife, Martha, settled on Panther Creek, four miles north of McMinnville. They lived on the land in a shanty for four years before building this house on property that Newby donated to the town. Their house was just 200 yards from Newby's mill. (CI.)

Looking east from Baker Street down Third Street, this photograph was taken early in McMinnville's history. A couple strolls across unpaved Third Street. A peddler's wagon is in the center background, and flags waving above the street suggest a holiday celebration or gathering. (CI.)

Samuel Cozine operated a blacksmith shop where Linfield College now stands. At Newby's suggestion, Cozine moved his trade next to the Newby Mill. This location provided a steadier business as farmers visited while their grain was milled. The Cozines built a house nearby. (LI.)

Mahala Cozine was born about 1829 in Missouri, but she came west with her husband, Samuel, and settled in McMinnville. She was baptized in August 1846 at the Amity Church of Christ. She died in 1908 in Yamhill. The Cozines donated 20 acres of land to McMinnville (Linfield) College, including the Oak Grove, the site for Pioneer Hall, and Cozine Creek. (LI.)

Most McMinnville residents will recognize the Cozine house at Third and Adams Streets. Seen here about 1895, the property is now occupied by the McMinnville Downtown Association. (DA.)

Starting about 1851, riverboats provided transportation up and down the Willamette and Yamhill Rivers. Boats stopped in Dayton and, with higher river levels in the winter months, McMinnville. Riverboats were in use until about 1900, when rail and automotive transportation became prevalent. (CO.)

Dr. James McBride, an early Yamhill County physician, traveled great distances to see patients who could pay him only with provisions. Later, he became the first superintendent of public instruction in the Oregon Territory and was appointed by Pres. Abraham Lincoln as minister to the Hawaiian Islands. McBride died in 1876. (SL.)

Mahala Miller married McBride in 1830. Arriving on the Oregon Trail in 1846, the McBrides brought with them nine children and had five more after settling in Yamhill County. Mahala died on February 23, 1877, at 65 years of age. (SL.)

Two

LINFIELD

One could say that McMinnville has always been a college town. When the city was but a suggestion from William T. Newby to Sebastian Adams, school was always part of the plan.

Newby invited Adams to build a house near his mill along Cozine Creek so he could open a school with Adams as its teacher. To that end, Newby donated five acres along an old Native American trail to establish McMinnville College. The two men, along with Dr. James McBride, became founders and trustees of the college. Newby built the shell of a very large L-shaped building for a school, but Adams only lasted about a year before he found he could not support himself as a teacher.

The two men offered Newby's five acres and large building to the Baptist denomination as long as it was maintained "on a college level." McMinnville College was born in 1858, when the Corvallis Association of the Baptists met for the first time and accepted the offer.

The beginnings of the school were modest: five teachers and a few students charged between $6 and $10 per term. There were no commencement ceremonies in those early days; tough pioneer life demanded that most students quit before finishing their course of instruction. The college did not graduate its first student until 1884, when John H. Smith obtained a degree. Finances were very tough in those early days, as well. Students could get $2 off rent by bringing their own stove or providing a cow. Teachers were paid sporadically, and the college often seemed on the brink of going under.

In 1906, things began to turn around for McMinnville College, with the appointment of Rev. Leonard W. Riley as president. Riley increased the operating budgets, the college endowment, and academic standards. Members of the community donated more land, which allowed for the construction of more buildings. Then, in 1922, Frances Linfield gave a large financial gift, providing firm financial footing for the school and a new name in honor of her husband, Rev. George Fisher Linfield.

Today, Linfield College is a nationally recognized institution with 47 majors in three programs (and a distinctive international emphasis), campuses in McMinnville and Portland, eight satellite locations, and online degree programs for adults.

This large L-shaped building was constructed in 1855 and housed the entire college until Pioneer Hall was built in 1882. The L-shaped building was razed in 1893. (LI.)

Rev. George C. Chandler (left) was elected college president in 1858. He served until 1862. At the time, 44 students were enrolled. John W. Johnson (right) became president in 1864 and served three years. He was a popular teacher, and enrollment more than doubled, to about 104 pupils. Johnson eventually became president of the University of Oregon. (LI.)

Pioneer Hall was dedicated in 1883. The structure cost $25,000 and was the sole campus building for many years, comprising dormitories, classrooms, laboratories, a chapel, apartments for the president's family and some teachers, a library, and a music studio. It was built without water, electricity, or plumbing. (LI.)

The Young Men's Christian Organization (YMCA) was organized by I.D. Wishard on the campus of McMinnville College in 1887 and, by 1904, had 58 members. Member John E. Hale remarked, "The great thought that permeates the association is the symmetrical training of the spirit, mind, and body. From the YMCA come the bright, healthful, broad-shouldered, all-around men." (LI.)

On May 6, 1887, a group of female students and faculty members gathered on the McMinnville College campus to form a chapter of the Young Women's Christian Association (YWCA). Belle Johnson was the first president. The group held missionary study classes on Sunday afternoons, and members devoted themselves to "deeds of charity." (LI.)

The first years for the college were difficult, in terms of leadership and financing. Facilities were lacking, and debt was high. This photograph features much of the student body, presumably on the steps of Pioneer Hall, around 1891. During this time, Emanuel Northup arrived and became one of the most beloved professors in college history. He was paid only $650 per year but stayed for 44 years. (DA.)

William Newby donated five acres of land in 1855 to erect a school. When his denomination was not interested in creating a college, Newby offered the land to the Baptists. In 1855, they transferred a total of 10 acres and a large building to the college. This photograph was taken on opening day in 1892. (LI)

The Linfield College (formerly McMinnville College) class of 1926 returned to campus in 1951 for its 25th class reunion. The campus had changed much in the intervening years. By the time these alumni returned, the college's assets had grown to around $6 million, with 43 active faculty members, 20 of whom held a PhD, compared with only 2 in 1931. Tuition fees had also increased from about $75 to $250 per semester. (LI.)

The Linfield Observatory was completed in 1894 at a cost of $2,500. The A.W. Kinney estate donated the six-inch refracting telescope for the observatory. Kinney served on the college's board of trustees from 1874 to 1879. The observatory was scheduled for demolition when expansion became necessary, but instead it was renovated and used as a music practice room. (LI.)

McMinnville College began offering women's athletic curricula in the 1890s, as depicted in this photograph where coeds pose with weights. Women's basketball was also very popular although not always supported, even by college leaders. In early years, men were not allowed to attend women's basketball games. (LI.)

This 1896 photograph depicts students in the chemistry laboratory. Before 1906, McMinnville College had only four departments: collegiate, preparatory, commercial, and music. Enrollment at that time totaled around 175 students. (LI.)

The 1904 football team was one of the last before the tragic, accidental death of a player in 1906 disbanded the sport for many years. Then president Riley had been an avid football player until "modern methods" were employed in the game, including gang tackling. Riley said, "I think too much of my face, my limbs, and my life to run risk of having them ruined in any such game as that." (LI.)

In this 1904 photograph, students pose before Pioneer Hall. At that time, McMinnville College stood at a crossroads. With the college beset with debt and possible closure, Rev. Leonard W. Riley accepted the job as president in 1906. By extensive fundraising efforts, Riley brought the college out of debt within 10 years and served until 1931. During Riley's tenure, McMinnville College expanded locally and regionally and advanced from a junior college to an accredited institution. In 1922, the institution's name changed to Linfield College. (LI.)

The May Day celebration at McMinnville College began in 1904. The May queen was crowned by the court bishop, and the court bard would recite poetry. The annual tradition lasted for 65 years. In 1969, May Day was deemed no longer relevant to a generation preoccupied with the Vietnam War. (LI.)

Members of the Lambda Lambda Sigma sorority went to some length to create this photograph in 1909. The 14 young women posed with their heads poking through editions of the *McMinnville Telephone-Register*. The mission of the sorority was "for social improvement and clean, wholesome college fun." The first known sorority was founded in 1851 at Wesleyan Female College in Macon, Georgia. (LI.)

Members of the McMinnville College men's basketball team worked harder after practice than during—cutting wood and building a fire to heat water for their showers. Members of the 1911 team pose together holding the team ball. At one point, a team slipped away without consent to play in another city. Not only did the team lose, but members had to appear at chapel to apologize. (LI.)

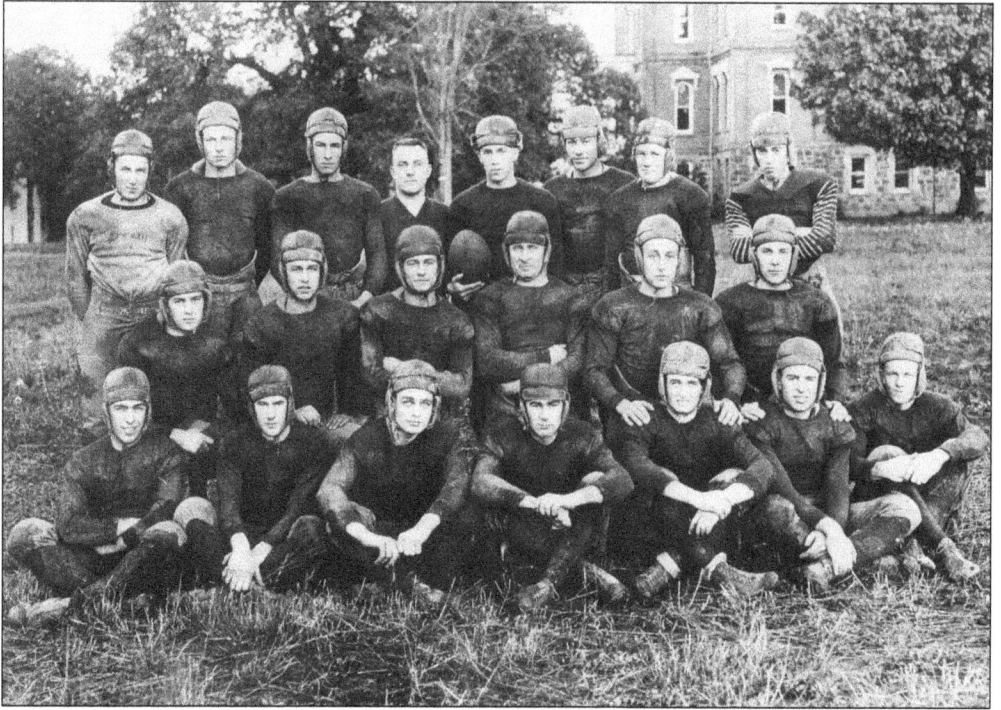

In 1922, football returned to Linfield College, under coach Maurice E. Pettit, a former student. The team lost the conference championship in 1924, subsequently joining the newly formed Northwest Conference. Other members were Whitman, Willamette, Pacific University, the College of Idaho, and the College of Puget Sound. (LI.)

It took many years to work out the relationship between the college and the City of McMinnville. In the 1870s, boarding students had become a local industry. By 1928, relationships had improved—as evidenced in this photograph where the McMinnville Chamber of Commerce presents a check for $27,646.30 to college treasurer Charles Kopf (right) to help to pay for a building program at the college. (LI.)

Melrose Hall contains the main administrative offices for Linfield College. It was completed on February 1, 1929, at a cost of $200,000—made possible through a donation by M.C. Treat. The name was chosen because it reminded Treat of a cloister in Scotland. Former Linfield president Leonard Riley and his wife, Julia, are buried beneath the northeast corner of the building. (LI.)

The 1934 college track team had more than races to worry about. Amid the Great Depression, just having enough to eat was a challenge. During that period, coach Henry W. Lever could always be counted on for a good meal when funds ran low. Coach Lever served from 1930 to 1949. (LI.)

The Service, Patriotism, Understanding, Responsibility, and Sacrifice (SPURS) Group has been a tradition at Linfield College since 1922. Founded as a women's service club, it is dedicated to community service activities, and members must maintain a 3.5 grade point average. The SPURS went coed in 1976. This particular group depicted is from the 1930s or 1940s. (LI.)

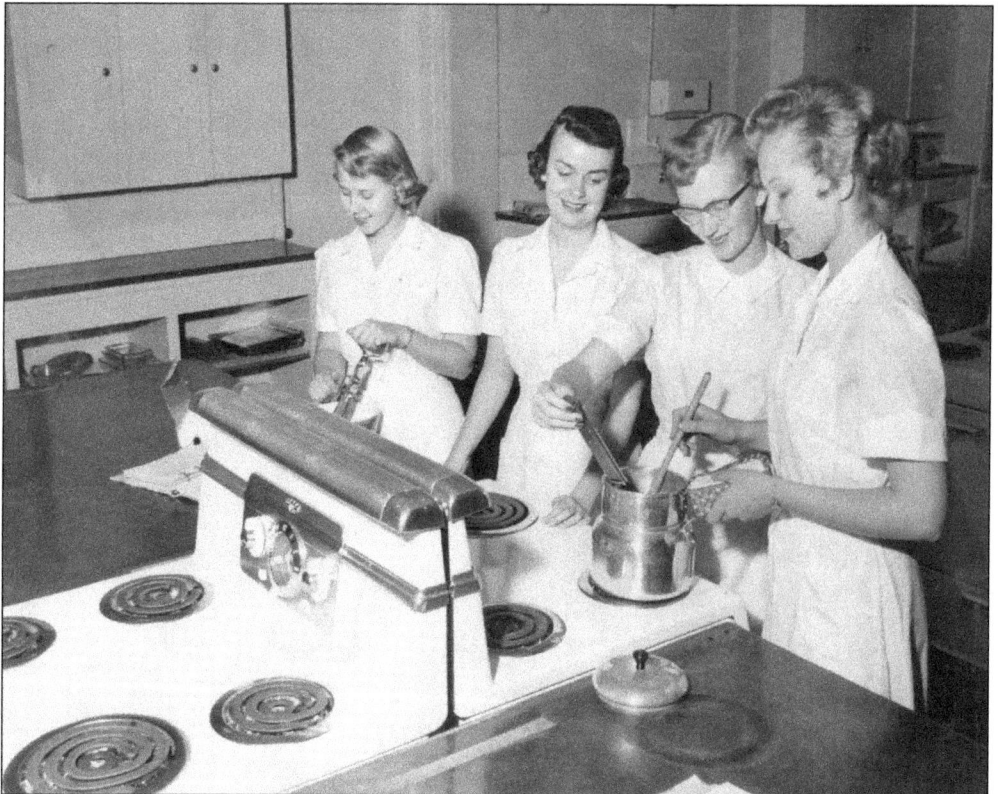

This photograph of a home economics class appears to have been taken in the 1940s. Roberta Simonsen (a Linfield alumna) wrote a book called *The Role of Home Economics in a Changing Society* in 1970. In 1947 and 1948, the Home Economics Department at Linfield College offered a day care program to serve the large population of parents who enrolled in college after serving in the war. An area of Pioneer Hall was set aside for the center. (LI.)

Two female students are seen here practicing their fencing technique in 1945. During the war, enrollment dropped to fewer than 200 students, and 85 percent were women. That year, many renovation projects took place and the college broke ground on the 16-bed Cook Memorial Infirmary, named for James H. Cook, a loyal Linfield college athletic fan and McMinnville physician. (LI.)

In 1946 and 1947, the Linfield College campus underwent many changes, as a close inspection of this aerial photograph shows. Pioneer Hall was completely rebuilt on the inside, at a cost of $130,000. Latourette Hall housed 37 female students. The music hall and chemistry building underwent remodeling, as did as a 2,200-seat stadium-dormitory on the west side of Maxwell Field. (LI.)

After World War II, there were 376 veterans on campus, in addition to the nearly 200 wives and babies. Although conditions were crowded, classes continued. Many former Portland Air Base buildings were moved to the college, including a theater, single-family dwellings, and the wings of the science building, which once served as a mess hall. Pictured here, Vera Beth Weidner shows a sloth skull to her 1948 class. (LI.)

Ken Trolan (left) and Walt Dyke studied physics together at Linfield College. Years later, they were both physics professors. At the Linfield Research Institute, in the basement of Melrose Hall, Dr. Dyke successfully developed a megawatt field emission cathode that allowed advances in communications, X-ray technology, and other vacuum-tube uses. (LI.)

Three

BUSINESS AND INDUSTRY

McMinnville's first business venture was the gristmill William T. Newby constructed in 1853. Newby came from a family of millers and, by 1853, recognized that the village could support a local gristmill for processing grain into flour. He traveled to Oregon City, purchased a millstone, and transported it back to the village by water raft and sled. There, next to the site of today's public library, he completed construction of the gristmill, which ended villagers' arduous, 80-mile journey to and from the mill in Oregon City. Two years later, Newby sold the mill to new owners to pursue other business. From that first commercial building, a city was born. After the mill was built, Newby donated adjacent land to encourage additional growth. Samuel Cozine set up a blacksmith shop, and Dutch Berry opened a store. By 1866, McMinnville had five stores, three blacksmith shops, two wagon shops, one photographer, two doctors, two churches, and, of course, the gristmill.

Once the railroad connected to McMinnville in 1872, the number of residents and businesses expanded and, by 1900, the population reached 1,420 people and the downtown was well established. Brick buildings—many of which remain to this day—began to replace wooden structures.

Before 1884, McMinnville citizens had to travel to Portland to do their banking, often buying goods while there. To provide residents an incentive to shop locally, McMinnville merchants sought means to open a local bank. At the time, the Wortman family was intending to open a bank in Lafayette but chose McMinnville instead, after merchants offered a brick building at the corner of Third and Davis Streets, where they opened the First National Bank (now KeyBank). As more businesses opened and more farmers produced crops, the need for another savings and loan emerged. The Yamhill County Bank (which became McMinnville National Bank) stepped in to fill that niche.

Some business opportunities grew out of difficult times. In 1893, a depression forced J. Frank Martin to band together with some other men to form the Oregon Fire Relief Association. Martin's job was to ride his bicycle across the county signing up customers. By 1895, the company expanded to eight Oregon counties and one day became Oregon Mutual Insurance Company.

One of the biggest changes in McMinnville businesses occurred shortly after the turn of the century. In 1903, the first automobile was purchased in Yamhill County. What started as a trickle soon turned to a flood, and by 1912 the city had to pave Third Street. The lively trades of livery stables and blacksmith shops slowly gave way to car dealerships and service stations.

Before he died in 1884, William T. Newby, who had already given the city so much, had expressed his wish to provide the town with reliable water. In 1888, a group of businessmen declared and fulfilled his wish, and the next year the city approved Ordinance 87, authorizing the construction of a water and electric system. McMinnville Water and Light was born, the first of its kind in the West.

This building was originally known as the Douglas Hotel. In 1896, George Washington Hendershott purchased it and built a home next door for his family to live in. The hotel was located next to the McMinnville train depot. Traveling salesmen and medical practitioners plied their trades for short stints from rooms within. (CO.)

Around 1900, automobiles were scarce in McMinnville, and many residents got around on bicycles or by horse and buggy. This photograph was likely taken around 1903. The First National Bank sits in the background, next to Jackson Irvine's Grocery Store on Third Street. Next door was J.H. Henderson's Family Grocery, which opened in 1903. In 1904, Irvine moved his store next to the post office. (CO.)

Elsia Wright owned and operated the McMinnville Harness Factory, located at the corner of Third and F Streets. In 1893, he constructed the Wright Building at the corner of Third and Davis Streets. At street level, he sold harnesses and farm implements. Notice the wooden horse in this photograph, which likely served as a mannequin for his wares. The building also housed a boiler that heated nearly all of Third Street. (CI.)

Taken between 1889 and 1903, this photograph shows McMinnville Bank at the corner of Third and Cowls Streets. The *Telephone-Register* office is to the left (with awning), as is City Market, with two pigs hanging on a rail outside the store. Next door is the shoe store belonging Sterling Harding, father of *Telephone-Register* publisher Frank S. Harding. The town jail and city hall are further to the left. (NR.)

First National Bank was founded by Jacob Wortman in 1883. It took nearly a year to get the bank ready for operation, including shipping a strongbox and vault door to McMinnville. The building at Third and Davis Streets was remodeled in 1911 and replaced with a new building in 1964. (KB.)

In the 1960s, when the First National Bank of McMinnville needed renovation, owners Frank (left) and Ralph Wortman decided to turn their temporary bank into an old-time general store. They displayed Frank's locomobile, a steam-powered car from 1902, and an old fire hose wagon, along with other articles from McMinnville's early days. (KB.)

McMinnville was given a $10,000 grant by the Carnegie Corporation on January 6, 1912, to construct a library. It resulted in a 5,120-square-foot library building. A 14,800-square-foot addition was completed and opened to the public in 1982. (CI.)

The Houck Milling Company built this five-floor feed mill and retail store at 855 NE Fifth Street in 1892. Charles B. Buchanan purchased the store in 1918. Alec Cellers joined the firm in 1924, and it became known as Buchanan-Cellers. Valley Feed and Supply purchased the business in 1979. This photograph appears to have been taken sometime in the 1930s. (CI.)

Raphael Jacobson built the large brick building on the northwest corner of Third and Davis Streets for $16,000. He sold dry goods, including clothing, shoes, carpet, linoleum, and window shades. William T. Macy had a successful furniture business next-door. The Macy's Funeral Parlor was located in the back of this store. The building was demolished to make way for US National Bank. (MA.)

An interior view of the William Macy Furniture Store reveals couches typical of the late 19th century, as well as wood chairs, upholstery/drapery fabric, rugs, and stools. Furniture in the store was made in Portland and shipped to McMinnville. William Macy served as the Yamhill County clerk and later became mayor of McMinnville. (DA.)

William Dielschneider apprenticed with McMinnville's first jeweler in 1888. In 1892, Dielschneider purchased the store and broadened the selection to include diamonds, vest chains, watches, fountain pens, clocks, and silverware. William's younger brother, Francis, joined the enterprise in 1896. In 1900, watches sold for between $1 and $25. (NR.)

Pleasant P. Wright was born in Oregon in 1872 and operated a confectionery shop between 1900 and at least 1923 in McMinnville. The shop was located at 421 Third Street. A 1904 advertisement reads, "Chocolate chips. Everybody is fond of chips. We have made up a fine assortment for this week's special. A good carpenter is known by his chips. So also is a good confectioner to carry out this idea." (DA.)

The Hotel Elberton, managed by Thomas A. White, opened in 1905. The hotel immediately became a popular meeting place for McMinnville residents and visitors. White prepared dishes in the hotel restaurant using ingredients from his nearby farm. (CI.)

This photograph of the Hotel Elberton's lobby was taken August 1919. Harry (center) and Tom (left) White stand ready to help customers. The man on the right is unidentified. Rooms at that time cost between 75¢ and $1. There is also a sign over the counter encouraging tourism to Pacific City. (DA.)

The Hotel Elberton, built originally with two floors, was the most elegant hotel in town at the time, with 26 rooms, a barbershop, cigar store, and ladies parlor. Third and fourth floors were added in 1910. In 1932, with the addition of an elevator, came a name change to the Hotel Oregon. The Hotel Oregon at 310 NE Evans Street is currently owned by the McMenamins. (NR.)

This February 1938 photograph features the old McMinnville Post Office at 414 NE Evans Street. McMinnville's original post office opened on May 29, 1855, with Elbridge Edson as postmaster. It was set up in the drugstore of Dr. Horatio Van Veighton Johnson. Mail would come by horseback once a week. The postmaster would read names aloud as recipients stepped forward to receive their letters. (CO.)

The Wells-Lamont-Smith (originally Wells Lamont, per sign) Corporation opened a glove factory in McMinnville in the mid-1930s at Second and Baker Streets. By July 1938, the plant employed 175 workers who cut, sewed, and formed cotton and leather gloves. Minimum wage at the time was only 30¢ per hour. The town competed with other Oregon cities to get the factory located in McMinnville; payroll at the time totaled about $2,200 per week. (CO.)

The Wells-Lamont-Smith glove factory worked at capacity in July 1938. The sewing room employed 110 women who sewed while inspectors checked over the finished products before gloves were shipped out nationwide. The company also had factories in Iowa, Missouri, Illinois, and Minnesota. (NR.)

In the shipping department of Wells-Lamont-Smith, inspectors made sure that the finished products had no flaws. Much of the plant operated on a per-piece basis. New workers were slower and often did not produce enough to make the minimum wage (30¢ per hour). Company records showed that many workers made at least 10¢ more per hour than minimum wage once they were proficient. (NR.)

Despite the Great Depression, employees at the Wells-Lamont-Smith factory enjoyed an abundance of work. During the 1930s, the company opened seven factories, including the McMinnville plant. New equipment installed tripled production capacity and nearly doubled the number of workers. Although it is unknown if she is in this image, Garnet Payne worked at this factory at the time this photograph was taken. (NR.)

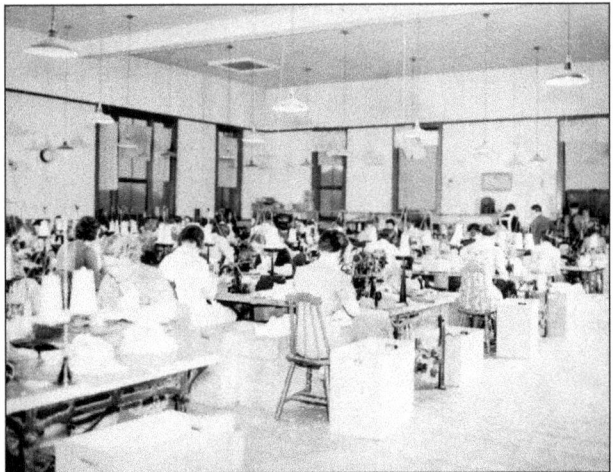

The Shell Service Station at Third and Baker Streets featured a crew of 10 men, shown here in a 1947 photograph. Standing at far left is owner Herman A. Larsen, and owner Gale Vinton is at far right. The crew was described as "well trained, efficient, and always dapper in clean uniforms," providing "personalized service, tailored to individual needs." (LA.)

Larsen and Vinton obtained the dealership for Buick, Pontiac, and GMC trucks in 1944. The pair delivered the first vehicle to Oscar C. Yocom Sr. in 1946. The building pictured is located at Second and Evans Streets and was at one time a livery stable. When Larsen and Vinton were setting up the building, they discovered an old airplane in a second-floor room. (LA.)

The Gilbert Tilbury Company started in a livery stable and began selling Model T Fords in 1911. The first automobile came to McMinnville in 1903. By 1912, there were so many cars that the city had to pave its streets. By the early 1920s, there were no more livery stables in McMinnville. This photo was taken in the early 1940s. In 1950, Tilbury took on partner Chuck Colvin. (NR.)

The Gilbert Tilbury Company was awarded the Mercury franchise in 1952. This photograph was taken in honor of that event. Pictured from left to right are (first row) Ray Jueneman, a longtime salesman and owner of a bar in Carlton; and unidentified; (second row) unidentified, and Gilbert and Beulah Tilbury; (third row) Jim Burford, and Chuck Colvin. (NR.)

Charles B. O'Dell owned a well-known tire store in McMinnville in the 1930s. O'Dell became known for his tire recapping machine, which he purchased for the then extravagant price of $2,000. O'Dell boasted in a *Telephone-Register* advertisement that his recapped tires featured "Tire value at its best. Economy and safety all combine in the construction of this tire." O'Dell drew business for his recaps from all over northwestern Oregon. (NR.)

In the 1930s, the purchase of a new freight truck was big news. Robert R. Rand stands by the latest edition to the Rand Truck Line, with an International truck, one of 10 in his fleet. The truck was said to average 7.5 miles per gallon and was "Firestone Equipped . . . another saving!" The advertisement in the *Telephone-Register* was sponsored by the Courtemanche Hardware & Implement Company. (NR.)

Stanard Grocery was a well-known market in McMinnville during the 1930s. Art King, pictured here on January 28th, 1937, cuts up turkeys in his meat market located in the store. A *Telephone-Register* article about King states that at this time he had been butcher for a decade and had once plied his trade at the Peoples Market along Third Street. (NR.)

Stanard's Grocery store was located at the corner of Third and Cowls Streets and was very popular during the 1930s. Owned by H. Wayne Stanard, the store boasted four deliveries each day and took cash-on-delivery orders. Note the simple phone number (314) on the side of the delivery vans. (NR.)

Laundry services began in McMinnville as early as 1888, with the opening of the McMinnville Steam Laundry operated by William Lambert. There were two Chinese laundry houses located on the edge of town on Adams Street. By 1910, Lambert picked up and delivered laundry to area homes. This 1937 photograph shows the A.K. Montgomery Home Laundry service truck. The business phone number is 47. (NR.)

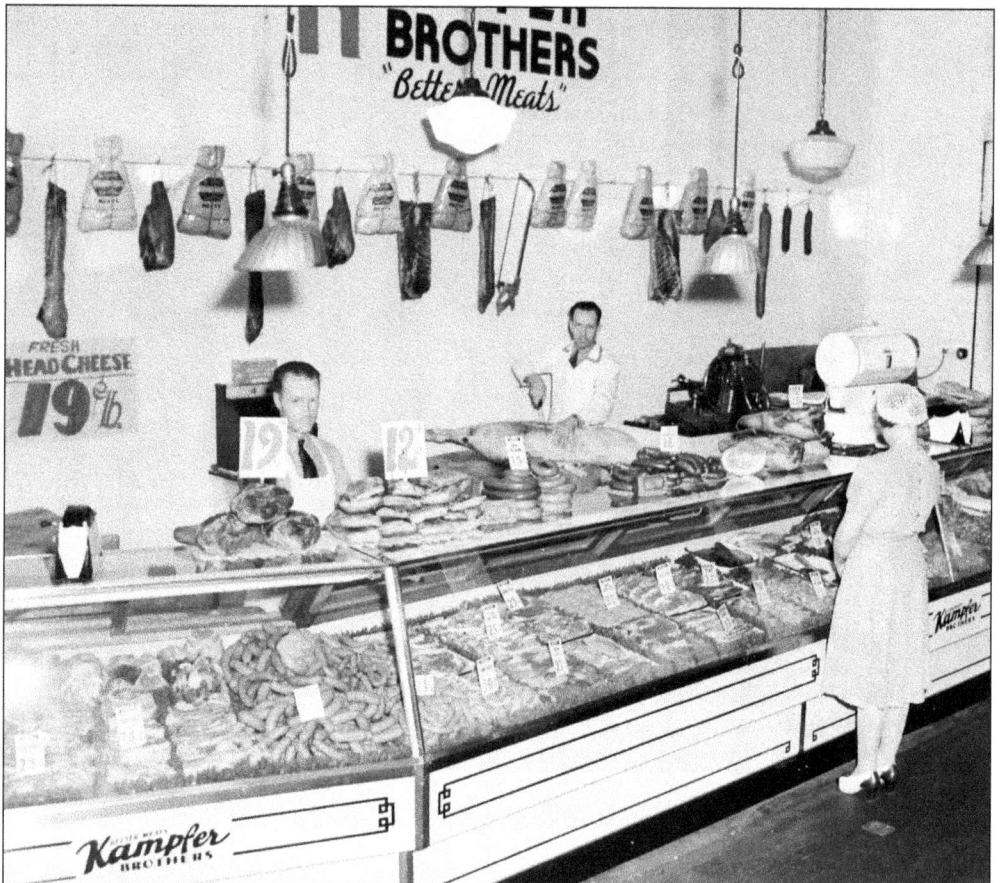

Butcher shops in McMinnville date back to at least 1870, when Adolph Matthies opened his shop on the south side of Third Street between A and B Streets. Often, there were four butcher shops stretched out along Third Street. The competitive nature of this particular industry forced many of the shops to close. This 1940 photograph shows the Kampfer Bros. Meat Market counter. (NR.)

Ernest. V. Blair opened and managed the J.C. Penney Store in 1920. He was president of the Kiwanis Club and president of the chamber of commerce. This photograph was taken in June 1939, as Blair shows off a newly remodeled millinery department. The story in the *Telephone-Register* was part of a series titled "Know Your Businessman." (NR.)

The prices for meat in the 1940s were presented prominently in the meat counter at Gill's Meat Market in McMinnville. Steak sold for between 42¢ and 65¢ per pound, sausage sold for 49¢ per pound, and it appears that ground beef sold for about 36¢ per pound. (NR.)

Manager Harold Nichols described his brand-new Richfield "superservice" station as having "only the latest devices for the quickest and most efficient service to customers." The station, located at Baker and Fifth Streets, cost $11,900 to build and was in addition to an $8,000 bulk oil plant already in operation. Services included wash, polish, and lubrication services. (NR.)

In addition to bottling all Pepsi products, the Scovells also produced Mission soft drinks and Hires Root Beer. They installed coin-operated machines throughout the county and shipped Pepsi all the way to Lincoln City. Pictured from left to right are George Scovell, Pat Scovell, and Edna Scovell. Pat and Edna Scovell purchased Yamhill County's only bottling plant on Third Street in McMinnville in the 1950s. (Courtesy of Susan McGregor.)

The Nestlé's Milk Products factory is listed in the 1914 and 1920 list of companies in McMinnville. The plant produced, among other things, condensed milk. In 1927, the *Register-Guard* in Eugene ran a story about this product coming from McMinnville, along with "new recipes" about its use. The plant closed in 1953, and this was one of the drivers for a renewed effort to bring industry back to the city. (NR.)

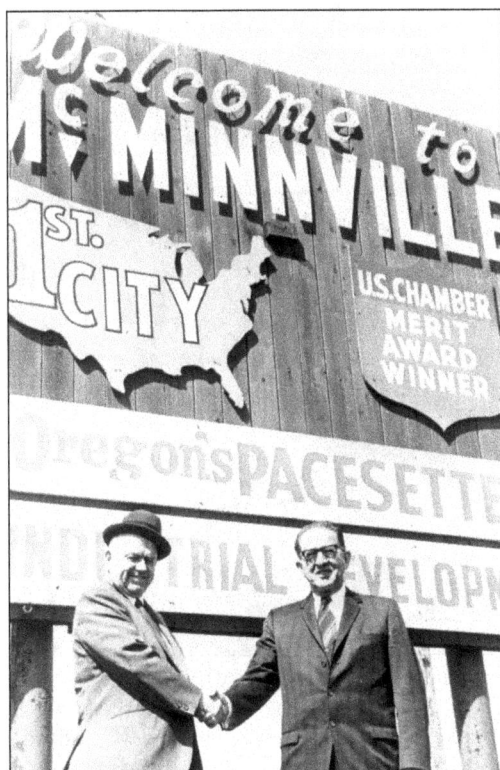

McMinnville had the honor of being named a "1st City" by the US Chamber of Commerce. As part of an industrial promotion, Chuck Colvin (left) and Rudy Windeshauer stand in front of a billboard constructed to mark the designation. The McMinnville Industrial Promotions Organization had a campaign to locate nine industries in 1969. The success of the campaign led to the award. (CO.)

In 1903, William T. Macy and his brother, Walter, purchased a furniture store and funeral parlor in McMinnville. The funeral parlor was in the back of the store. Furniture merchants were often connected to the coffin trade because they had access to wood products and tools. The coffins were made locally. Pictured here is an 1880 Rockfalls hearse. (MA.)

In the early 1920s, the Macy brothers closed their furniture store and moved the funeral parlor to Second and Evans Streets. Although the Macys had a funeral parlor, it was common for embalming to take place in the home. Funerals were also commonly held in homes. Undertakers wore black and a big black top hats. This Lippart-Stewart hearse was built in 1913. (MA.)

The present Macy & Son Funeral Chapel was built in 1936. This photograph was taken in the 1950s. After World War II, Glen Macy joined the family business. Macy described it as "a 24-hour-a-day job." Between 1975 and 1982, Glen's sons Steve and Scott joined the firm. Today, the fifth generation carries on the responsibilities of the family business. (MA.)

On September 9, 1948, the FCC issued a permit for a radio station in McMinnville on Lafayette Avenue. KMCM went on the air on June 18, 1949, when Mayor Rudolph H. Windisher threw the switch. Brothers Jack and Phil Bladine were the original owners of the station, as well as, respectively, publisher and editor of the *Telephone-Register*. In 1951, KMCM's slogan was "Yamhill County's listening habit." The station is now known as KLYC. (NR.)

Farnham Electric was established in 1920 by Leslie Farnham. Ralph Farham started working for his brother Leslie in 1928; once World War II started, he took over running the company while his brother served. This picture was taken in the 1940s outside of the store at 546 Third Street. Ralph is pictured second from left, and his wife Marie is holding a small girl. Sitting on top of the truck are daughter Dian Farnham (right) and son Waldo Farnham (center). (FA.)

By 1960, Farnham Electric had grown considerably. With the company's trucks parked out front, the staff has gathered for a photograph. Shown are, from left to right, Hugh Bernards, Fern Bensen, Bonnie McGill, Les Woodard, Darrel Parnell, Waldo Farnham, Jerry White, Leslie Farnham (Ralph's brother), Percey Carlson, John Dobkins, and Ralph Farnham. According to the *Daily News-Register*, the company wired houses, performed electrical repairs, and sold "automatic electrical appliances." (FA.)

The truck on the far left in the background of this photograph is called "a line foreman's dream" in the October 20, 1938, addition of the *Telephone-Register*. The vehicle was designed and built by a McMinnville Water and Light lineman and engineer. It was called "as handy and useful as a can-opener in a housewife's kitchen." (WA.)

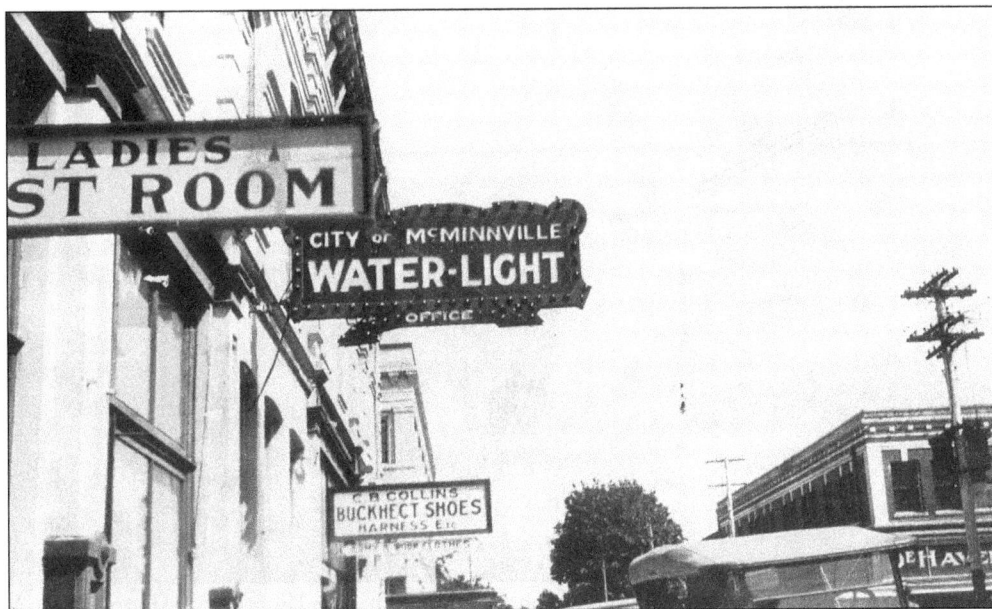

Every evening until 1889, the city lamplighter filled and lit lamps powered by kerosene on posts located on street corners. Citizens used wells and cisterns for water. By 1923, McMinnville Water and Light had offices at Third and Cowls Streets and provided electric power service and clean water originating from high in the Coast Range. (WA.)

The Baker Creek Power Plant was built in 1910 in response to the growing demand for electricity. It was equipped with the latest technology, including three General Electric 2,500-volt transformers, at a cost of $3,157.40. The plant used 1,500 cords of wood during the first year of operation. (WA.)

For much of its early history, McMinnville Water and Light produced electricity by burning wood. The generator in this photograph was located at the Baker Creek plant. Eventually, the city used hydroelectric as well as diesel fuel to produce power. This plant also used a 300-horsepower Corliss steam engine that the city purchased after rejecting a bid by Portland General Electric to provide power to McMinnville. (WA.)

In 1938, McMinnville Water and Light had 19 employees, including Paul Jones, pictured here overhauling a cylinder at the municipal power plant. This type of maintenance included grinding down the cylinder walls of the diesel generator. The new diesel plant helped McMinnville Water and Light surmount debt and operate at a surplus. (NR.)

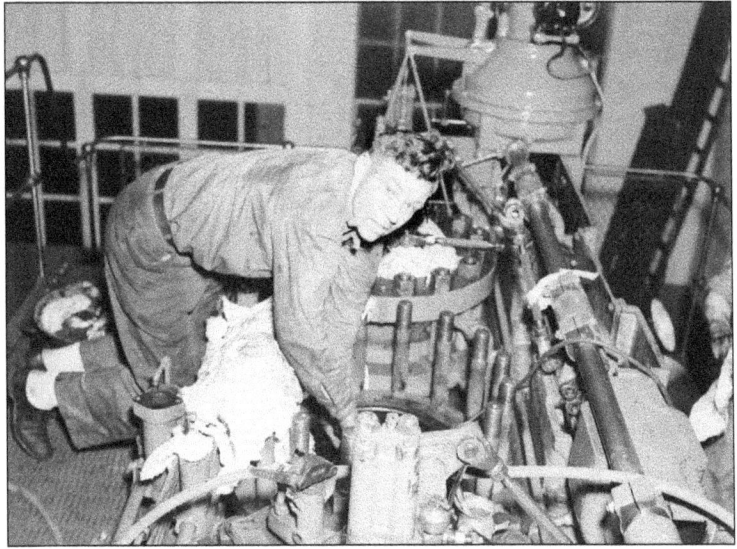

McMinnville Water and Light began in 1889 and produced electricity for over 50 years. When this first electric plant began providing power to Third Street, the idea of electric power generation was only seven years old. The first plant, pictured here, stood on the banks of the South Yamhill River. It supplied 1.5 million gallons of water, beginning on December 10, 1889. (WA.)

The McMinnville Water and Light diesel generator shown here was expensive to purchase, operate, and maintain. Buying more generators to meet increasing power demand may have factored into the decision to supplement, and then replace, locally generated electricity with that produced by the Bonneville Power Administration. (NR.)

In October 1938, crews from McMinnville Water and Light are pictured installing power poles. That year, the power company acquired a 1,800-horsepower diesel engine and became one of the largest diesel power plants in the United States. Just 10 years later, the city purchased all of its power from the Bonneville Power Administration. (NR.)

Walter S. Link served on the McMinnville Water and Light commission for over 30 years. The 1900 census shows his profession as bank vice president, but in 1906, he worked as a cashier at the McMinnville National Bank. The Water and Light commission named the Walter Link Dam after him. The dam, on Haskins Creek, supplies water to the city. (MS.)

William J. Brower became water superintendent in April 1910. Brower is sitting third from the left. John Dixon, a fishing friend, sits to Brower's right. Brower's first job was to supervise the digging of a well on Baker Creek. Bad-tasting and -smelling well water led the commission to Haskins Creek, high in the Coast Range, for a long-term supply of clean, dependable water. (WA.)

In 1923, this electrical generating plant was built at the corner of Fifth and Irvine Streets at a cost of over $60,000. It had three diesel generators and kept the city from having to purchase power from outside. Once the city began to use Bonneville power, this plant was no longer needed. In 1989, it became home to Panther Creek Cellars. (CO.)

Linemen Mike Marsh (left) and Art Clevenger perch on top of the transformers at the McMinnville Water and Power electric plant located at Fifth and Irvine Streets to perform maintenance. Once in operation, the plant managed to supply the needs of the city for only two years, and the city had to make an emergency purchase of more generators. (WA.)

Four

AGRICULTURE

Early in its history, McMinnville was known as "the most flourishing village in the county." In many areas of the Willamette Valley, the first settlers needed to work the land to provide for their families before they could begin a trade for wages. A gristmill was in place by 1853. In addition to wheat, early crops included berries, fruit trees, hazelnuts (filberts), grass seed, and sweet corn. Livestock was also raised, primarily beef cattle, sheep, and turkeys.

By 1938, turkeys began gobbling up sales in McMinnville. A barbecue tradition was started to celebrate McMinnville's turkey industry. Called Turkey Rama, the celebration continues, but in recent days more as a community event. Turkey farms and the turkey processing plant disappeared in McMinnville. However, other livestock production continued, and by the 1950s the area around McMinnville boasted some 150,000 acres of land and livestock in production, the latter expanding to include veal, lamb, and pork.

In 1966, the nature of McMinnville agriculture changed again. David Lett planted a vineyard in the hills outside Dundee and in 1970 purchased a former turkey processing plant to house a winery. Although wine-making in Oregon goes way back to 1847, Lett pioneered a rebirth of the industry. In 1979, his 1975 South Block Reserve pinot noir shocked the world by placing in the Top 10 at the *Gault & Millau*–sponsored Wine Olympics competition in Paris. That event sparked an industry that has since gained worldwide fame—all from a winery still located in McMinnville.

Today, the top agricultural industries in McMinnville include fruit and nut production, nurseries, grains, and vegetables and melons. Although filberts have long been a major crop, McMinnville used to be known as "Walnut City" for the 100,000 walnut trees growing in the area. The Columbus Day storm of 1962 nearly wiped that industry out in a single day. Cattle ranching, sheep and goat farming, and poultry and egg production also rank high.

Although not identified, this photograph is probably of the Isaac Lambright threshing crew. Some of the men seated in the front row hold a pitchfork. Female crew members supplied food for the men, and it appears this vehicle was the "chow wagon." The owner is identified on the side as "Nichols Dry Goods & Groceries" of Dayton. (DA.)

Threshing wheat was a community project in the 19th century. Isaac Lambright was well known in McMinnville as the president of the Star Flouring Mills. He also owned extensive fields of wheat, such as the one pictured here. Lambright was a stockholder in the US National Bank. This photograph of the Lambright threshing crew was taken in 1887. (DA.)

Hops were first grown in Oregon in the late 19th century. By 1880, Oregon was known as a hops market. Picking hops was a family tradition. This photograph shows members of the Schreiber family in 1911—including aunts and grandparents, though individuals are not identified. (UL.)

Dorothy Blenkensop, granddaughter of Martin Schreiber, picked hops near McMinnville during high school from 1935 to 1938. Although Dorothy is not identified in this photograph, whole families were known to pick hops during the Depression. It was hard work, but Dorothy looked forward to the camaraderie of working with cousins and friends. The family picked during the day and camped in the fields by night. (UL.)

The women at work are unknown, but Dorothy Blenkensop described life at the time. She said picking hops started early, at 7:00 a.m. Beginning any earlier made the hops too heavy with dew. Pickers were paid only once, at the end of the season. Dorothy worked at DeLashmutt's Hop Yard and Wood's Yard in Dayton. She remembers eating peanut butter and onion sandwiches and drinking from the community water barrel. At night, they sang around a campfire. (UL.)

Hops grow up long poles. During picking, the poles were let down to the picker's waist, where the small tasteless flowers were pulled off the vines and into canvas baskets. When a basket was full, it was weighed, and the picker's card stamped. During picking season, many families stayed in small cabins that had no showers and toilets. Outhouses were down the road. (UL.)

John Redmond purchased a 340-acre farm in Yamhill County, southwest of McMinnville, in 1874. He was the first person in the county to breed stallions, and he greatly influenced the stock-raising industry in the state. Redmond, originally from Ireland, fell in love with the American West and was a member of the Cumberland Presbyterian Church. (MS.)

The original John Deere tractor dealer in McMinnville was DeHaven Tractor & Implement Company. The store opened in 1941 at the corner of Third and Cowls Streets. Here, employees pose in front of the business beside various pieces of farm equipment. William DeHaven owned the Commercial Livery Stable at Evans and Fourth Streets in the 1890s. His son, also William, ran a hardware store in 1930. (SL.)

In this 1939 photograph, three women pick cherries at the Hillcrest cherry orchards. These cherries were destined for a new local product—to become maraschinos. Although in many states cherries are picked by machine, the tradition of handpicking cherries remains in Oregon. After picking, the cherries are transferred to boxes for transport. (NR.)

Boxes of cherries inside the Wright Walnut Drier plant were barreled in a sulfur-dioxide solution for three weeks before being graded, bleached, and sent to a manufacturer. This plant was the first large-scale cherry producer of its kind in the area. The crop had a value between $50,000 and $60,000. (NR.)

About 2,500 barrels of cherries from the Eola and Hillcrest orchards sit in rows outside the Wright Walnut Drier on Lafayette Avenue. In 1937, when this photograph was taken, the production of maraschino cherries were rare in the United States. The 16 workers at this plant hoped some of these cherries would be of a grade high enough to become maraschinos. (NR.)

From this perspective, workers on top of the cherry barrels are visible outside the Wright plant. There are 250 pounds of cherries per barrel. After they were stored, the cherries were graded by running them over belts. Some were stemmed and pitted. (NR.)

Pictured here is Stuhlfeier's Nut Plant as it appeared in the *Telephone-Register* newspaper in the 1940s. The side of the building indicates that the plant handled walnuts and filberts grown in the many orchards around McMinnville. During this time the city was known as Walnut City. An *Oregonian* article in 1939 quotes the local saying "Nuts to you," referring to the walnut industry. (NR.)

Female employees of Stuhlfeier's Nut Plant sort through filberts to be processed in the plant. In 1939, the *Oregonian* reported, "During the last 15 years great quantities of filberts have been added to the annual nut harvest." This photograph was taken for a *Telephone-Register* newspaper article. (NR.)

The second annual Pacific Coast Turkey Exhibit was held in McMinnville in December 1939. The event included the grand champion in the "Dressed Bird Division," a 36-pound tom turkey entered by Harry F. Williams, a Yamhill turkey man and county commissioner. More than 400 birds were entered into the competition. Both attendance and the number of entries set records that year. (NR.)

The front page of the McMinnville *Telephone-Register* in December 1939 proclaims, "Turkey Named Grand Champion." The caption of this photograph reads, "Some of the world's finest turkeys were entered into the second annual Pacific Coast Turkey Exhibit here Wednesday and today. Charles H. Wilson, Newberg, chairman of the county turkey committee, and Mrs. George Webster, Dayton, member of the committee, display the prizewinning yearly Bronze tom entered by Mr. and Mrs. Miles Maxwell, Dayton." (NR.)

The caption for this photograph in the December 7, 1939, edition of the *Telephone-Register* reads, "An added attraction at the banner show was this exhibition display of royal palms by Mr. and Mrs. Paul McDowell, of Hillsboro. Tim Derr, prominent McMinnville turkey man, is pointing out features of this new breed to Robert M. Caldwell, a sheepman, and Mr. Derr's neighbor on Three Mile Lane." (NR.)

Brownie, an eight-year-old collie, looks disinterested as owner Joseph Greenhoot receives an award from Betty Jean Cox, Miss McMinnville, in 1949. Brownie was named the top turkey-herder after a competition comprising eight other turkey-herding dogs. Joseph received a "fine trophy," according to the *Telephone-Register*, and Brownie got lots of good-tasting dog food. (NR.)

Five

NEWS-REGISTER

Family-owned since August 1928, the *News-Register* dates its newspaper family tree to 1866, through four branches and a long line of publications. A brief overview of names and dates does not do justice to the spirited newspaper operations and colorful early journalists of Yamhill County. Suffice it to say that, together, they chronicled the rich history of early development for McMinnville and Yamhill County.

For much of this historic overview, thanks go to the late George S. Turnbull, University of Oregon professor of journalism, for his 1939 book, *History of Oregon Newspapers*. Three involved mergers. The *Yamhill County Reporter* was the county's first newspaper. It began as the *Lafayette Courier* on January 1, 1866 and was founded by J. H. Upton. It was sold, moved to McMinnville, renamed multiple times, and, in 1872, became the *Yamhill County Reporter*. The *McMinnville News* was first published in 1901; the paper was founded by O.G. Estes. The *News-Reporter* was created in 1905 from merger of the *McMinnville News* and the *Yamhill County Reporter*. The *Oregon Register* was founded in August 1881 by W.M. Townsend and S.R. Frazier in Lafayette. *West Side Telephone* was founded by publishers Talmadge and Turner on June 15, 1886, in McMinnville. The *Telephone-Register* was created February 1, 1889, from a merger of the *West Side Telephone* and the *Oregon Register*. The *News-Register* (today called *Yamhill Valley News-Register*) was created on February 12, 1953, when the *Telephone-Register* purchased the *News-Reporter*.

Lars Bladine of Iowa purchased the *Telephone-Register* in 1928 with his eldest son, Jack, who came to McMinnville that year to run the newspaper. Lars came to McMinnville in 1932 and was publisher until his death in 1941. Jack took the reins until his early death in 1957 at age 52. His brother, the late Phil Bladine, became publisher, and passed that title to his son, Jeb Bladine, 34 years later in 1991. By then, all four Bladines had served as president of the Oregon Newspaper Publishers Association while continuing the *Telephone-Register*'s strong tradition of community journalism.

This wooden building, located on the west side of what is today Cowls Street, mid-block between Third and Second Streets, housed the *Telephone-Register* beginning in 1889. Directly south along those wood sidewalks was the McMinnville Fire Department bell tower, and the town jail was next door. The building may date earlier as a newspaper building, since the *Telephone-Register* was a merger of the *West Side Telephone* and the *Oregon Register*. (NR.)

This brick structure at Fourth and Evans Streets was built about 1920 to house the *Telephone-Register*. The newspaper staff is pictured outside the building after receiving a large shipment of paper. The *Telephone-Register* merged with the *News-Reporter* in 1953 to form the *News-Register*. The building is now identified as the Old News-Register Building. (NR.)

Lars E. Bladine became a leader in state Republican Party politics and served as president of the Oregon Newspaper Publishers Association. He died suddenly of a heart attack in 1941, two years after the *Telephone-Register* was named the nation's best weekly newspaper. (NR.)

Jadee Johnson, who managed the *News-Register* sheet-fed printing business during the 1950s and 1960s, gained local renown when he and friends played an early-morning golf game every day for a year. The printing division, later named Oregon Lithoprint, expanded into Portland with the acquisition of Bridgetown Printing Company. During the 1990s, Oregon Lithoprint sold its sheet-fed business and built a new coldset web-offset printing plant off Riverside Drive in McMinnville. (NR.)

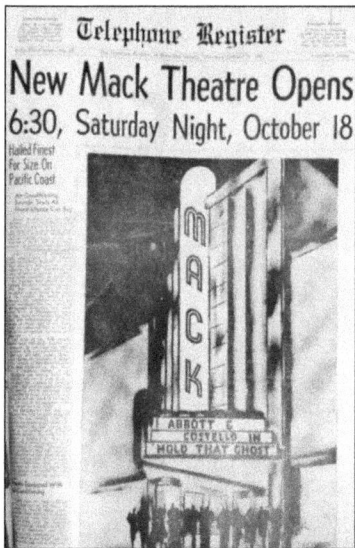

Telephone Register

New Mack Theatre Opens
6:30, Saturday Night, October 18

Hailed Finest
For Size On
Pacific Coast

The October 18, 1941, opening of the Mack Theatre in downtown McMinnville drew a "special section" in the *Telephone-Register*. Headlines boasted, "Hailed Finest For Size On Pacific Coast," and touted air-conditioning, a sound system, and seats. It seemed like a variation of the city's nickname, but the name actually came from the first and last two letters of the owners' names: Mathias W. and Robert J. Mattecheck of McMinnville. (NR.)

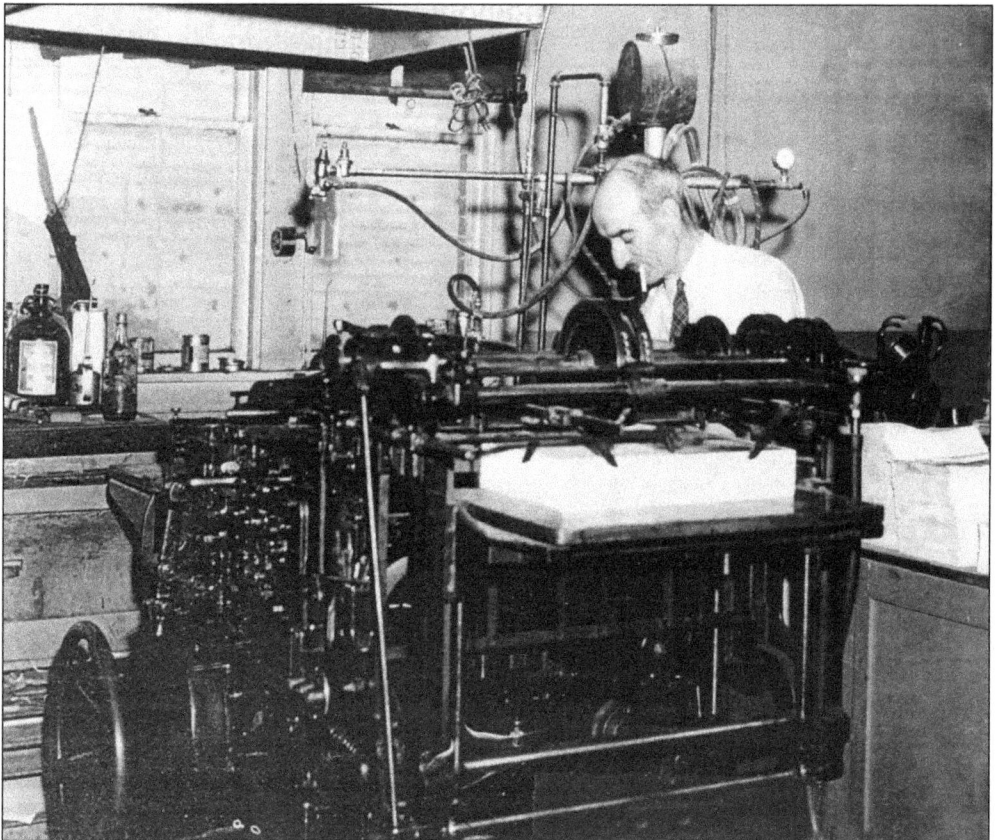

Printing was a companion business for the *Telephone-Register* newspaper since it opened in 1889. Letterpress, linotype, and rotary newspaper press operators helped produce the newspaper while providing printing services for local businesses and residents. Ade Lowe, pictured working in the back print shop, started with the *Telephone-Register* in 1943 and retired in 1959, which was when the newspaper converted from hot type to cold offset printing. (NR.)

72

This Goss rotary press, installed during the late 1930s, improved quality reproduction and increased printing speed. The equipment, pictured here with a pair of unidentified pressmen during the 1940s, delivered paper from a continuous roll, a 19th-century advancement over single-page printing from centuries past. This press was removed in the late 1950s, when the renamed *News-Register*, *Hillsboro Argus*, and *Forest Grove News-Times* built a new coldset web printing plant in Hillsboro. (NR.)

The linotype machine, operating like a slow-motion typewriter, revolutionized typesetting speed when it was introduced in 1884. These machines were in the back shop of the *Telephone-Register* and *News-Register* until the late-1950s. Linotype operators were skilled tradesmen whose keyboard dexterity set individual lead castings of movable metal type into place on large trays of type and images. (NR.)

The *Telephone-Register* float in McMinnville's 1951 downtown parade depicted how the printing office would have looked when the newspaper opened in 1889 after the merger of the *West Side Telephone* and the *Oregon Register*. Standing atop the float is press operator Ade Lowe. Young boys jogged alongside, passing out handbills with a replica of the newspaper's first edition on one side and the latest edition on the other. (NR.)

John B. "Jack" Bladine (left), eldest son of Lars Bladine, came to McMinnville from Iowa in 1928 to take control of the *Telephone-Register*. Lars moved to McMinnville in 1932 with his wife, Inez, and younger son, Philip N. "Phil" Bladine (right). Jack became publisher after Lars died in 1941 and was joined by Phil as editor. Phil became publisher when Jack died in 1957 at age 52. He died in 2008. (NR.)

Six

COMMUNITY

A city is more than just a collection of buildings. It is made up of the people and dynamic relationships that make a community. As McMinnville linked more to the outside world through stagecoaches, steamships, rail, and highway, more people were drawn there, and the community grew. The greatest percentage-growth period for the new city was between 1895 and 1910. Many of the two- and three-floor buildings downtown were constructed then. Businessmen built grand homes in ever-expanding neighborhoods. The period's growth was largely influenced by rail transport that started in 1872. Opportunities abounded as locally produced water and electricity flowed into this fast-growing city. Remarkably, Third Street of the 19th century is not that different visually from that of the early 21st century.

The first municipal water and light plant in the western United States facilitated many changes to businesses and homes. The newspaper even held meetings to teach women how to cook on an electric stove.

Much of the heavy labor to build McMinnville's infrastructure came from immigrants, mostly Chinese, who worked for little money and, regrettably, suffered harsh treatment and discrimination. To provide for themselves, the Chinese built an underground support system, the remnants of which can still be seen today under some downtown buildings.

The automobile also changed the landscape of McMinnville life forever. Speed laws were created, and police had to enforce them. Early developers of the city were left to designate streets as they saw fit. It got so confusing that even longtime residents had problems finding their way around. In 1928, a city ordinance forced 75 name changes to McMinnville streets, to unify names. Travel by automobile was dangerous until the West Side Pacific Highway opened in 1923. In 1912, a public library was built and an Elks lodge formed; the city's first swimming pool opened in 1918, and parks soon followed. Cultural groups formed, including literary societies, performing artists, and theater works.

A deliveryman sits on his wagon in front of Jackson Irvine's Grocery Store on Third Street. This photograph was taken in 1890, with Hendrick Grocery next door. Near that time, Marion Hendrick advertised three cans of tomatoes for 25¢ and "choice Maine corn" at 10¢ a can. By 1911, all traces of Jackson Irvine and his business had disappeared. (CO.)

This photograph is believed to depict George W. Jones' lumber store. The sign reads, "Lumber, Sash, Doors, Mouldings." Jones reportedly had a sash factory at the western foot of Third Street in 1898. A newspaper article states, "(They) have furnished the materials that have been used in the construction of public buildings in McMinnville." (DA.)

A construction crew digs out a basement of the future Taylor-Dale Hardware Building (608 NE Third Street). Across the street stands the Overland Car Agency. Known as the O'Dell Building, it was also used as a gas station and warehouse. Later, it became the headquarters of the McMinnville *News-Register*. It was built in 1904 and renovated in 2000 at a cost of $400,000. (CI.)

In 1884, Thomas Kay returned to McMinnville after studying at the Baptist college (Linfield College). He formed a partnership with Charles Bishop and opened Bishop and Kay Tailor and Clothier. Bishop married Fanny Kay and went to work for his father-in-law at the Thomas Kay Woolen Mill in Salem. He later owned and operated the Salem Woolen Mills Store in Salem and purchased the Pendleton Woolen Mills. (DA.)

McMinnville's first high school building stands in the background of this early city photograph (left center). It appears that electric poles are going up around town, but it is not clear whether the wires had been strung. The caption on the photograph states, "Partial view McMinnville, Ore." (CI.)

Charles Bishop departed the partnership with Thomas Kay in 1888. Kay then partnered with a Mr. Todd, and the store became Kay and Todd. In 1894, Thomas Kay went to work for his father at his woolen mill in Salem. Kay served on the city council and school board in McMinnville. Later he served in the Oregon Legislature and 14 years as state treasurer. (DA.)

This view was taken from the old courthouse building facing southwest. Commercial Livery (left) stood at the corner of Fourth and Evans Streets. James Henry and a Mr. Gates opened the livery in the 1880s. An advertisement from 1898 states the stable was "well equipped, being supplied with the best stock, buggies, and carriages in the city." (DA.)

Clark Hamblin arrived in McMinnville in the summer of 1900 and opened a men's clothing store in the Union Block Building on the corner of Third and Davis Streets. Dell Wheeler bought into the store two years later, and the store became Hamblin-Wheeler Clothing Company. The building also had space for dentist and physician offices. This photograph was taken in 1920. (DA.)

This early view of McMinnville shows the train station in the right foreground. George Washington Hendershott purchased the Commercial Hotel in 1896. The hotel (far left) was originally known as the Douglas Hotel. The Hendershott home to the left of the train station now houses a French-style bistro. The county courthouse stands in the background. (DA.)

In 1906, Byron Brower owned a transfer business in McMinnville. He is visible in this photograph, appearing to have gathered his wagons along Third Street. Brower also hauled goods in his flatbed wagon. In the foreground on the left is a sign for J.W. Ballinger Auctioneers and Real Estate. (DA.)

Edwin Clyde Apperson started as a bookkeeper or janitor for United States National Bank in McMinnville but ended up as its president. Clyde and his wife, Alvis, built this home on Cowls Street in 1895. Apperson was treasurer for Linfield College and one of the founders of the Oregon Mutual Insurance Company. (Courtesy of Patti Webb.)

Alvis Apperson, who supervised the Apperson home on Cowls, was raised in North Carolina and was said to be very formal. She came to Oregon as a seamstress and was a Daughters of the American Revolution member. The Apperson home is protected as a significant historic resource by the City of McMinnville. (Courtesy of Patti Webb.)

The basement of the original Elks building, in the 500 block of Third Street, was once a Chinese restaurant. The restaurant was active from 1908 to 1920. The basement covers an area of about 9,000 square feet. The Chinese people who came to Oregon were forced into the most dangerous jobs and were generally mistreated. Until 1964, many Oregon cities, including McMinnville, prohibited Chinese residents from operating businesses within the city limits. (Courtesy of Christy Van Heukelem, photographer.)

Some Chinese residents operated brothels, gambling parlors, and opium dens, like this one, in the basement of the original Elks building. The basement also provided a place for traveling Chinese to sleep. A number of stoves, sinks, and washtubs used by the Chinese were also found in the basement area. (Courtesy of Christy Van Heukelem, photographer.)

Orange O. Hodson came to McMinnville in 1880. In 1888, he purchased his father's interest in the hardware business. In 1909, he built a hardware store at Third and Cowls. That store is seen on the right of this photograph. Hodson manufactured and installed much of the roofing and galvanized cornices seen on many downtown buildings. (DA.)

In 1905 and 1906, the McMinnville community put on the play *An American Citizen* by Madeline Lucette Ryley. Although there are too many names to list all, the young man leaning to his right on the second row is Isaiah Wortman. The *New York Times* said of the play, "The posture of events is oddly and whimsically contrived." (WO.)

Col. Jacob C. Cooper was a teacher, author, merchant, publisher, and commanded the Oregon Grand Army of the Republic (GAR). He was also a visionary and builder who designed and in 1899 constructed the large arch that crossed Third Street. Cooper was known as one of the most influential men in the state and was on the board of directors for the Lewis & Clark Centennial. (MS.)

The original Cooper Arch was constructed in 1899 at the intersection of D and Third Streets. The arch (actually a series of arches) was built to celebrate the 18th Annual Department Encampment of the Grand Army of the Republic of Oregon. The arch itself was some 20 feet tall. In the 1920s, it mysteriously disappeared from historical records. (DA.)

This photograph features a military processional preparing to march along Third Street. Many photographs of downtown McMinnville were taken facing east, but this one was taken facing west, with Courtemanche Hardware on the right. The photograph was probably made between 1907 and 1920. (DA.)

John Wortman purchased the first automobile in Yamhill County for his two sons, Ralph and Frank, for $500 in 1902. The locomobile was steam powered. Although Wortman bought the car in November, he could not bring it home until the next May, when roads were sufficiently dry. Frank is photographed in the driver's seat. A paved highway from Portland to McMinnville would not be completed for more than 20 years. (WO.)

This station was purchased by the railroad in July 1879 and was at one time the depot. The West Side Rail Line was McMinnville's first rail connection. Trains left Portland in the morning and stopped in McMinnville for lunch before continuing on to Corvallis. The two-story building had once been a hotel rumored to be a brothel. (CO.)

McMinnville may have had three train stations at some point in its history. This one survives along Third Street. The date is unknown, but a man in the photograph holds a banner for the McMinnville Elks Lodge. Waiting for the train used to be a big event, and residents would gather round with "two 10-cent sodas and a 5-cent bag of popcorn," according to barber Pete Maloney. (DA.)

86

In the early 1900s, automobiles were rare, so Ralph Wortman's "second Ford in McMinnville" was noteworthy. Pictured is his Model R. Only about 2,500 were sold. At a cost of around $750, it was called the Edition de Luxe. It had a four-cylinder, 15-horsepower engine. Wortman may have taken this photograph after a successful duck hunt. (CO.)

The paved highway from Portland to McMinnville was not completed until the 1920s. Back in 1910, automobiles were still a fairly new trend in town. Here, the Automobile Good Will Tour leaves Third Street for a journey to Eugene. It took this group of motorists two days to reach the Emerald City, 90 miles south. (DA.)

The automobile in this photograph appears to be a Ford Model T, driven by Ralph Wortman. Wortman introduced the automobile to McMinnville in 1905. Many car dealerships sprang up along the downtown stretch by the 1920s. By this time, a Model T could be purchased for a mere $295. (WO.)

Before the days of paved highways, most roads were simply dirt. During winter, these turned muddy, rutty, and nearly impassable. One solution used by early travelers from McMinnville to the coast was to build what were called "corduroy" roads. This one was built in the Coast Range around 1900 and featured thick planks placed side by side. (DA.)

A series of five lighted arches was erected above Third Street in 1914. The arches remained until the 1930s. This night photograph was taken in 1925. Businesses pictured include the Enna Jettick Shoe Company, the Palm Café, Rexall Central Pharmacy, a billiard hall, and the Lark Theater. (CO.)

Taken from Baker Street along Third Street, this east-facing photograph was probably taken in the 1930s. Montgomery Ward is on the corner, next to the Courtemanche Appliance Store. During that time, Archer Spencer and Charles Baker were managers of Montgomery Ward and were members of the McMinnville Rotary Club, chartered in 1921. (CI.)

The McMinnville Elks Lodge was charted in 1912. In addition to attending lodge meetings, members traveled around the state, renting an entire railcar, to take part in community events. During World War II, the facility was opened to members of the National Guard encamped near McMinnville. Elks members also manned the observation post atop the old courthouse. (Courtesy of Elks Club.)

In April 1888, Hiram Tucker deeded a 200-by-180-foot lot for a new Yamhill County Courthouse located in McMinnville. The courthouse covered an area of 9,000 square feet and served the county until it was demolished because of structural concerns. A new courthouse replaced the original building in 1964. (NR.)

Herbert L. Toney served as McMinnville's mayor in 1917 and 1918. He was active in the chamber of commerce, a trustee of Linfield College, and a member of the McMinnville Water and Light Commission for many years. Toney was also very active in Mason Union Lodge No. 43. Toney worked at First National Bank of McMinnville and First Federal Savings & Loan. (MS.)

On October 5, 1935, Herbert L. Toney conferred a master Mason degree upon W. Boyce Stanard at the Union Lodge of the Masons in McMinnville. Part of Toney's tenure as grand master was to encourage members to assist those out of work during the Great Depression. Toney died on March 3, 1946. (MS.)

In 1908, two years after establishing a park, the city built this auditorium at the site of the current aquatic center. It was billed as an all-purpose sports and events center. The enormous structure was torn down in 1922, and the parts were sold for salvage. The windows of the auditorium were used for a poultry house. (CC)

From 1900 to around 1915, McMinnville Water and Light encouraged consumers to use electricity for cooking and heating water. The *Telephone-Register* hosted meetings attended by over 2,000 women to teach them how to use electricity in the kitchen, like this demonstration held in the Lark Theater. As an incentive, Water and Light charged a flat rate for stoves and water heaters instead of the metered rate used for electric lights. (WA.)

This photograph of Third Street was taken on October 20, 1938, by the *Telephone-Register*. Courtemanche Appliances appears on the left, with People's Market on the right. A truck parked on the left side is from the Rand Truck Line, which operated between Portland and McMinnville. Cornerstone Coffee now sits across the street from the former Courtemanche location. (NR.)

Around 1953, Vinton and Larsen of McMinnville donated drivers education vehicles to Willamina, Yamhill, and McMinnville High Schools. Richard H. Schoenborn (left), driver instructor for Willamina High School, stands inside the door of the "dual control" vehicle, while Gale Vinton hands over the keys. The American Automobile Association also participated in the program. (LA.)

Saima Vinton created the name "Shodeo" by combining horse show and rodeo. The annual horse-dominated celebration was held from 1943 to 1962, overseen by the Yamhill County Sheriff's mounted posse. Dona Lee Greiner (Blensly) was chosen as Shodeo queen in 1950. (CO.)

McMinnville's first public swimming pool was installed in the city park near the Cozine Ravine. The kidney-shaped, outdoor pool was unheated. Next, the city built a second pool on the other side of the ravine, but pool renovation only lasted for about a decade. This photograph of the upper park pool was taken in 1953. (NR.)

Norma Hoffman served as lifeguard and swimming instructor for the McMinnville public pool during the late 1930s. The pool opened in mid-June and featured Red Cross swimming schools, water carnivals, lifesaving exhibitions, and competitive water sports. The pool was renovated in 1938, and the reopening caused quite a stir. (NR.)

In the mid-1950s, city recreation staff handled a park filled with kids all day during the summer—reading comics and playing checkers, tetherball, softball, and box hockey (pictured here). Children would snag crawdads in the little stretch of Cozine Creek that ran through the lower park. There was also free play, tournaments, and whatever activities the staff could improvise to keeps kids occupied and having fun. (NR.)

Ralph Wortman often drove his steam-powered locomobile around town for special occasions. One such event was the arrival of Dwight D. Eisenhower early in his tenure as president. Pictured here, Eisenhower waves gamely as Wortman drives him into oncoming traffic from the wrong side of the road. (CO.)

The buildings are familiar, but not the names, in this 1960s photograph of Third Street. Rutherford's is now Harvest Fresh Groceries. Kienle Music was open until at least 1978. In the 1950s, Swinney's Bakery (left) was a popular gathering place. (DA.)

On July 1, 1960, Joe Dancer (left) became McMinnville's first city administrator. Dancer served five mayors over a 28-year period. He grew up in McMinnville, worked at Buchanan-Cellers, owned a school bus company, and served one term on the city council before beginning work for the city. During his tenure, the Highway 18 bypass was completed and the city's population doubled. (NR.)

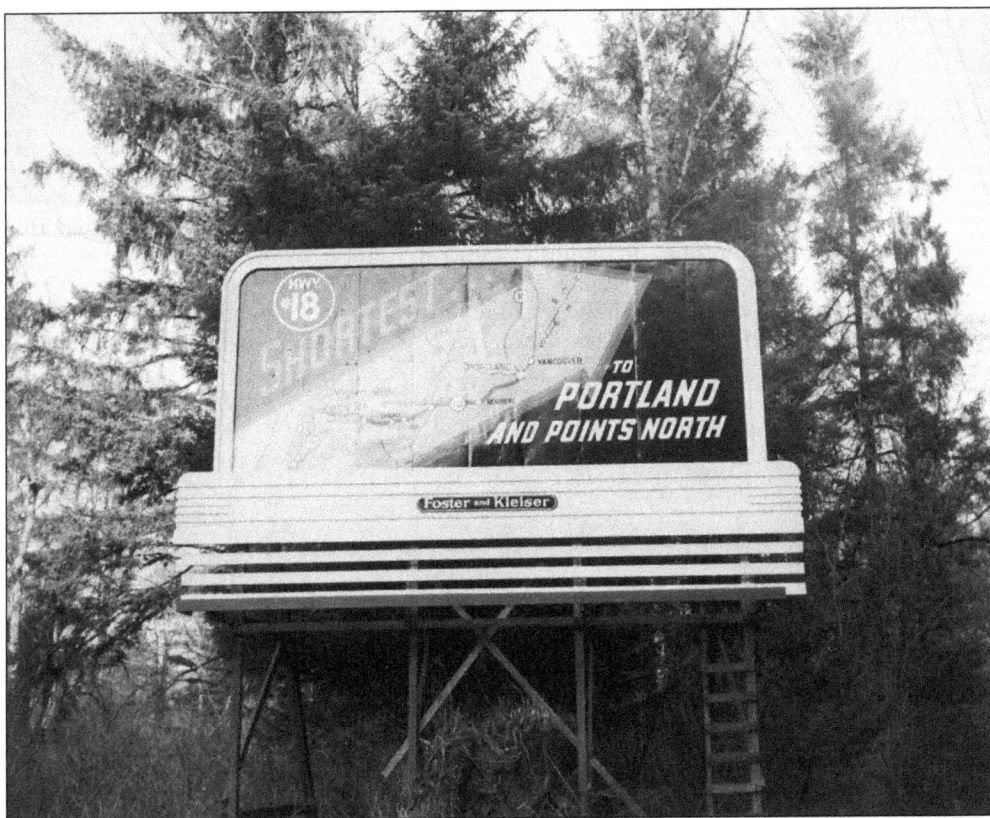

A little less than 10 years after the highway's initial construction, the McMinnville Chamber of Commerce purchased and installed this billboard near the then western terminus of Oregon Highway 18. The sign was designed to encourage motor traffic to come through McMinnville, describing the route as "shorter, safer, scenic." Highway 18 ended at McMinnville until 1963. (NR.)

A Columbus Day Storm hit McMinnville hard on October 12, 1962. The *News-Register* reported that this was the "worst storm to hit Yamhill County in history." By the next day, three people were confirmed dead and eight were injured. One of the fatalities was Walter W. Miller, who was hit by a beam while trying to cover hay in his McMinnville barn. Warehouses, barns, and cars were destroyed. The cab pictured was the victim of a tree felled by the high winds. (NR.)

Wind speeds reached over 100 miles per hour through McMinnville in the 1962 Columbus Day Storm. Many roofs and whole portions of homes were ripped off. McMinnville officials estimated the damage from the storm would top $15 million. At the height of the storm, Mrs. Robert DeGraff gave birth to a daughter under emergency lighting at McMinnville Hospital. (NR.)

The Columbus Day Storm knocked out communications between McMinnville and the outside world, as the *Oregon Statesman* noted. Thousands of trees were uprooted by the winds. This one appears to have just missed a house. The *News-Register* estimated that 175,000 prune and 50,000 walnut trees toppled in the storm. McMinnville had been known as the Walnut City before the storm, which destroyed half its walnut trees. (NR.)

On nearly every farm in Yamhill County (2,800 total), between one and eight structures were damaged or destroyed during the Columbus Day Storm, according to the *News-Register*. Some vehicles narrowly escaped damage, such as the one shown here. (NR.)

Norm Scott served five terms as mayor of McMinnville from 1967 to 1979. In 1974, he created the downtown committee on redevelopment. Instead of a mall, the committee recommended renovating Third Street by adding new streetlights, moving utility wires underground, planting trees, and rounding the sidewalks. Scott also served on the McMinnville Water and Light Commission. Scott passed away in 2008, and the water treatment plant bears his name. (CO.)

CITY HALL

McMINNVILLE DRAGWAYS

Presents

DRAG RACES
AUGUST 30-SEPTEMBER 13

AND

NHRA DIVISIONAL
DOUBLE POINT BONUS RUN

SEPTEMBER 27

LARGEST RACE OF THE 1964 SEASON
ALL TOP FUEL AND GAS DRAGSTERS

71 CAR CLASSES – – 12 CYCLE CLASSES

6 ELIMINATORS

ALL RACES HELD RAIN OR SHINE

TIME TRIALS 8:00 am to 12:00 pm   ELIMINATIONS 1:00 pm
Xmas Tree Starting, Dual Lane Chrondek Clocks, 40' Running Lanes, 5000 feet Long

SPONSORED BY

McMINNVILLE JC's   –   –   –   –   COLUMBIA TIMING ASSOCIATION

In the 1960s, drag racing became very popular in McMinnville. Many residents remember the McMinnville Dragway near the airport, which is now used for gliders. This poster boasts "the largest race of the 1964 season" and was sanctioned by the National Hot Rod Association. *Hot Rod Magazine* occasionally ran articles about the races in McMinnville. One 1964 event was sponsored by the Columbia Timing Association and the McMinnville Jaycees, which ran concession stands at the races. (CI.)

Seven

HEALTH AND
PUBLIC SAFETY

Two features important to a growing community are public health and safety. In 1874, McMinnville was a fast-growing town with many businesses and homes being built and then burning down because most were constructed with wood. Residents formed the Star Hose Company No. 1 and, when the fire bells rang, 15 to 20 volunteers would drop everything, grab a hand-drawn cart equipped with buckets and a few ladders, and head for the fire. They tried to douse fires using buckets of water drawn from wells. In 1916, the city purchased a motorized fire truck and began paying its first firefighter. In 1928, the city of McMinnville was the second community in the state to add ambulance services; Corvallis was first.

Police services began in 1888. Pete Peterson, known as "Big Pete," was the city's first uniformed officer. During World War I, Peterson oversaw the daytime operations of the department while John Venable served on the night shift. Together they were known as "Big Pete" and "Little Big Pete." The town's first druggist appears to have been Dr. Horatio Van Veighton Johnson, who also owned the first drugstore.

In the summer of 1888, McMinnville endured a smallpox outbreak that placed the entire town under quarantine from its surrounding neighbors Amity, Dayton, Lafayette, and Sheridan. McMinnville residents were not permitted to leave town, and infected residents were confined to a hastily built structure known then as a pestilence house. The outbreak resulted in at least one death. A quick response by doctors and town leaders was said to have saved many lives. By the late 1890s, McMinnville had several physicians, including Dr. William Vose, Dr. J.E. Bartel, as well as many others who stayed only a short time. Dr. James Cook opened an office in 1896 in the Jacobson Block of Third Street and practiced there until his death.

The first hospital dates back to either 1911 or 1915, when Dr. James Wood and Dr. Elmer Goucher bought a three-story house on B Street. There was no elevator, so patients had to be carried to surgery on a stretcher. In 1937, McMinnville Hospital opened with 29 beds.

The 1883 photograph shows members of the volunteer fire department. From left to right are (first row) George Snyder, Allen V.R. Snyder (newspapermen), and Walter G. Henderson (Yamhill County Sheriff); (second row) West Wallace (grocer), and David H. Turner (county recorder). (FD.)

McMinnville's city hall and fire station are pictured before 1900. Four firemen stand at the ready in front of two hand-pulled hose units. The city's horse-drawn pumper wagon appears to be in the other bay. It took as many as 10 men to race to a fire with the hose cart, which was replaced by motorized vehicles in 1916. (FD.)

Before motorized fire trucks, the McMinnville Fire Department had to pull its equipment by hand. Here, the crew poses with its pumper unit wagon on West Second Street at the site of Alpine Village in 1891. A crew of 12 attended this unit, which often had to be pulled up the city's steep hills. (FD.)

This photograph depicts the McMinnville Fire Department officers in 1916. Shown are, from left to right, (first row) Ersel Pearson (the elder brother of future fire chief Ivan Pearson), Lee Waugaman, Chief Bert Loban, Ed Pratt, and Frank Chown; (second row) Chester Caldwell, John Benefer, Roy Fink, Clarence Hendershott, Bill Hardwick, Donald Ringle, Billy Martin Jr., and George Manning. (FD.)

In August 1916, the McMinnville Fire Department took delivery of its first motorized fire truck. It was a Luverne hose and chemical fire truck. Ordered in May from the factory, the truck was vermillion, with gold lettering, and weighed 5,480 pounds. It cost $2,700, according to the September 1, 1916, *Telephone-Register*. Posing with the truck in front of city hall are the 1919 fire crew and its dog. Chief Bert Loban stands at far right. (FD.)

Job No. _1014_   Owner _City of Mc Minnville_

Model _Comb. Fire Truck_   Town _Mc Minnville_

                             State _Oregon_

Completed _Aug 18-16_   Sold _May 15-16_   Delivered _Aug 21-16 shipped_

Motor _6-B-_   made by   Beaver Motor Co - Milwaukee Wis

Ignition { Bob-Bosch magneto / Mod S Igniter   Bosch magneto Co - New York N.Y.
                                Connecticut Tel Elec Co - Meriden Conn
         Vacuum Feed 213   Stewart Warner Co - Chicago Ill

Tanks _20 gal Freus F. J._   "   Shotwell Hobart Co - Minneapolis Minn

Radiator _Oaltop Cellular_

Transmission _C Unit_   "   Detroit Gear Machine Co - Detroit Mich

~~Carburetor~~ ~~Sprockets~~ _Mod R-1¼-_   Schebler Mfg Co - Indianapolis Ind

~~Center~~ ~~Drive Chain~~ _A28-Apco_   Apple Elec. Co.   Newark N.J.

Steering Gear and Connections _K left_   "   Gemmer Mfg Co   Detroit Mich

Front Axle and Hubs _126 A_   "   Timken Detroit Co - Detroit Mich

Rear Axle and Hubs _C - 7-1-_   "   Torbensen axle Co - Cleveland O.

Springs _2x8x40-5½ front_ / _2/2/0/42-3½ Rear_   "   Harvey Spring Co - Racine Wis

Wheel Base and Weight _150 in_ / _5480 lbs_

Brakes _Stan Ext r Int._   "   Torbensen axle Co Detroit Mich

Chassis Frame _Stan 4½ Chan. F. J._   "   A. O. Smith Co   Milwaukee Wis

Tires _36x3½ Dem Single + Dual_   "   Goodyear Tire Co   Akron O

Fenders _Oval Crown Front_ / _Flat rear_   "   Saginaw Sheet Metal Co Saginaw Mich

Hood _Oval Top- 41 in_   "

Body _#14 ga. -1700 ft cap._

Lamps { #376 Headlight / 398 Searchlight / 213 Tail Lamp }   "   C. M. Hall Co   Detroit Mich

Color _Vermillion Red gold lettering_

Extra Equipment _Chemical Tanks-_
         1-40 gal Holloway Luverne   Northern Fire apparatus Co Minneapolis
~~Remarks~~   2-3 · Turrets
          auto Dav - Piping
          200 ft Chemical hose ¾ 3 ply ·   Goodyear Tire Co   Akron O
     Siren- 6" Elec -   Auto Stat Co   Rochester N.J.
     Lantern - 2 - F. D.   R. E. Dietz Co   New York
     Ladder - 2 - Roof +   Peter Pirsch Co   Kenosha Wis
     Speedometer - Mod-11   Stewart Warner Co   Chicago Ill
     Storage Battery #9/2-L H   Philadelphia Battery Co Philadelphia

This is the actual order form from the Luverne Manufacturing Company for McMinnville's 1916 hose and chemical fire truck. Every portion of the truck was detailed, including the motor, ignition, transmission, brakes, fenders, and lamps. Companies that manufactured parts for the truck were located in cities including Milwaukee, Detroit, New York, and Philadelphia. The Luverne Fire Apparatus Company was based in Luverne, Minnesota, and is now owned by Crimson Fire Inc., of Brandon, South Dakota. (Courtesy of Crimson Fire.)

The McMinnville Fire Department pauses for a photograph in front of its 1924 American LaFrance pumper truck. From left to right are (first row) Tom Erickson, John Sauter, Arnold Widness, George Kinney, Bunny Boyce, Roswell Rossner, and Charley Price; (second row) Don Fink, Harold Messinger, Sandy Brown, Melvin Phelps, Ralph Farnham, Lynn Triplett, and Carl Trent. (FD.)

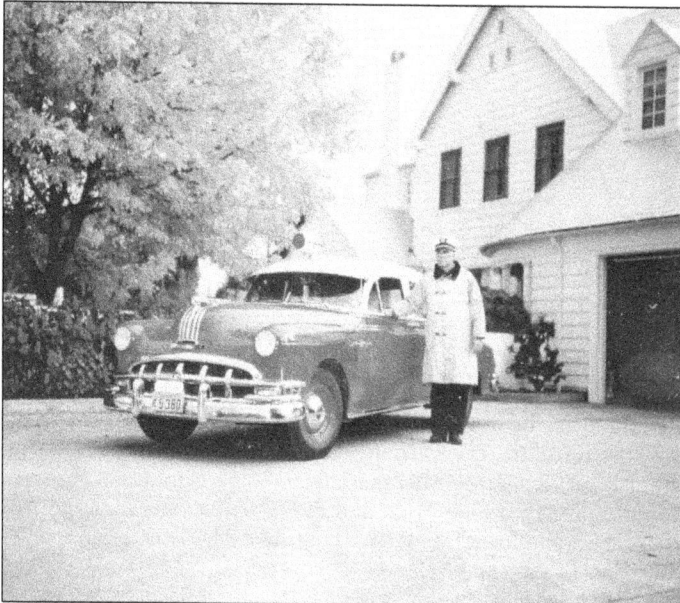

Ivan Pearson joined the McMinnville Fire Department in 1916 and later became the first paid fire chief. Pearson became nationally known as an expert in overseeing volunteer fire departments. He received many awards locally and nationally. After 49.5 years of service, he retired from the position of chief. In 1965, he became the city's first fire marshal, a volunteer post he held until his death in 1966. (LA.)

On May 17, 1938, fire broke out in the attic of the United States National Bank building on Third Street. The blaze began as a flue fire and caused an estimated $9,000 in damage. The smoke and water also damaged sugar, flour, and other goods in the Safeway store that occupied the building along with the bank. It took every firefighter in the city to extinguish the blaze. This photograph was taken facing south on Davis Street. (NR.)

On November 4, 1973, McMinnville High School's Wortman Stadium was destroyed by fire. Two days later, Michelbrook Country Club burned. Arson was suspected in both fires but not proven. Both structures were replaced within 18 months. Later, a man named Bob Howard admitted to setting 22 fires around McMinnville, including one at Thrifty Drug that injured six firemen. (FD.)

In 1928, the McMinnville City Council approved the purchase of the city's first ambulance, a De Luxe emergency car, for $3,245. Pictured here is the 1940s ambulance that most likely replaced it. McMinnville's fire department was among the first to merge ambulance service with the fire department, following the City of Corvallis. (FD.)

The jailhouse in McMinnville in 1892 looked more like a shack than a jail. The structure, including the county courthouse, was constructed in 1888 for between $62,000 and $70,000. The jail lasted until 1911, when Merrill Ruffner, incarcerated for disorderly public conduct, broke out and set fire to the jail. Ruffner escaped to California and even wrote a letter taunting the police. He was never caught. (Courtesy of Oregon State Archives.)

Ward Sitton was elected sheriff of Yamhill County in 1900. The next year, he poses with deputy William C. Hagerty in the sheriff's office, presumably in the Yamhill County Courthouse. Sitton was 50 years old when this photograph was taken. He was single and boarded with the Herbert Heath family in the south part of McMinnville. (CA.)

Glenn Shipman began work as an Oregon state police trooper in 1948. He was stationed in McMinnville. After he resigned, Shipman began working for the Yamhill County sheriff's office and in 1980 was appointed to complete the term of a sheriff who had resigned. Shipman later ran successfully for two terms and spent nine and a half years as Yamhill County sheriff. (Courtesy of Glenn Shipman.)

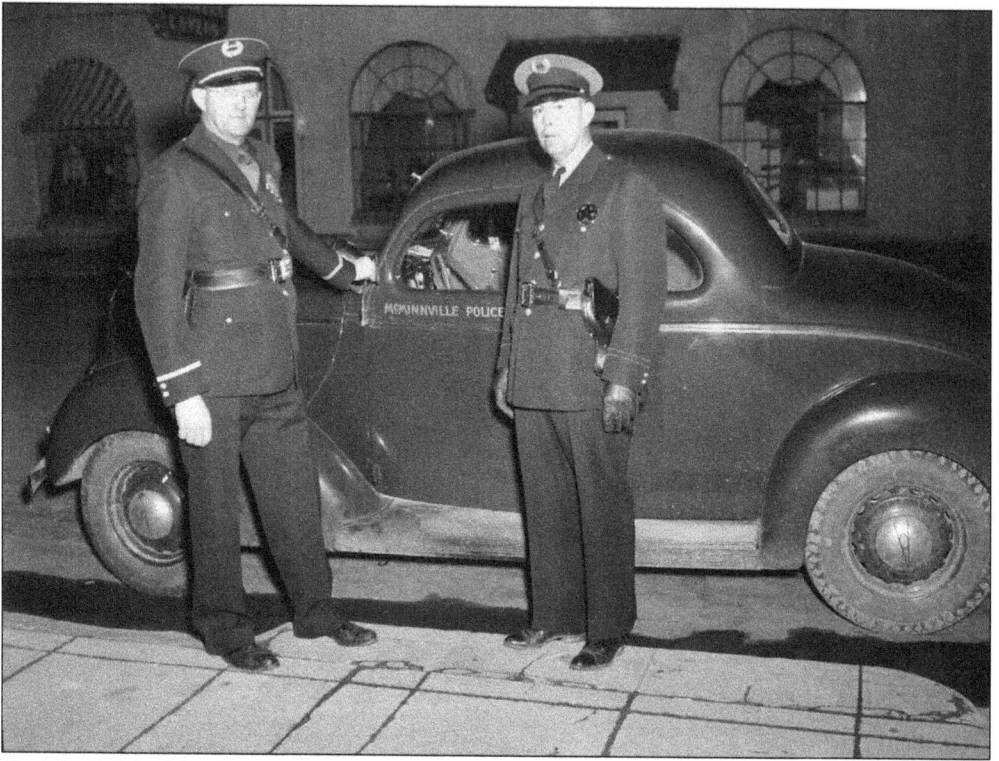

On March 24, 1938, the McMinnville Police Department got new uniforms and the event made front-page news and compelled Chief Ed Peterson (left) to park a patrol car on the wrong side of the street. Sporting a removable rubber top to his cap "to ward off the March showers," night officer H.E. Carr poses with Peterson. (NR.)

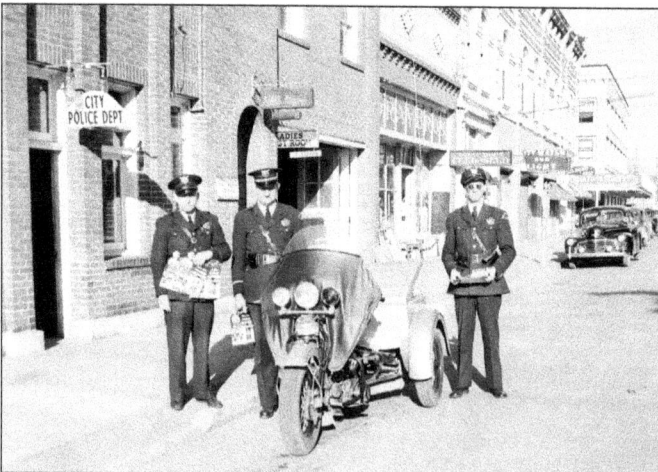

Members of the McMinnville Police Department promoted the March of Dimes campaign in 1948. The department helped distribute donation coin holders to local stores. Created by Pres. Franklin Roosevelt after his own struggle with polio, the March of Dimes funded vaccine research that ended the polio epidemic in the United States. (NR.)

Roy Brixy served as McMinnville's chief of police from 1957 to 1963. Before that time, there were no standards for police officer training. As part of the new Oregon-Washington Lawmen's Association, Brixy helped write House Bill 1590, the Police Standards and Training Bill, which was signed into law by Gov. Mark Hatfield on June 1, 1961, and created the Board of Police Standards and Training. (Courtesy of Nancy Law.)

Sgt. Mike Full of the McMinnville Police Department poses with Duke, the department's first K-9 patrol dog, for a November 17, 1982, story in the News-Register. Duke was credited with over 400 felony arrests during his career with the department from 1982 to 1991. He was used mostly for tracking purposes in narcotics investigations. (NR.)

On July 14, 1911, McMinnville's hospital was completed on B Street opposite Columbus School. The three-story wood frame building had 30 rooms, all opening to the outside. It was the only hospital between Portland and Albany. The operating room was reported by the *Telephone- Register* "to be fitted up with all modern appliances for the most delicate of operations." (CO.)

The staff of the new McMinnville General Hospital pose in front of the building. The hospital included a call-bell system so patients could alert the nursing staff. The building included offices for two doctors, as well as a surgical suite and treatment rooms. Bathrooms were in every patient room, which was an unusual feature at the time. (NR.)

McMinnville General Hospital was located on the corner of Fifth and Evans Streets. The 29-bed facility featured a solarium and a state-of-the-art communications system that allowed two simultaneous conversations outside of the hospital and three inside. Dr. John Manning was the primary doctor for the hospital, which also featured a delivery room and a nursery with six bassinets. The labor room was equipped with soundproof walls. (NR.)

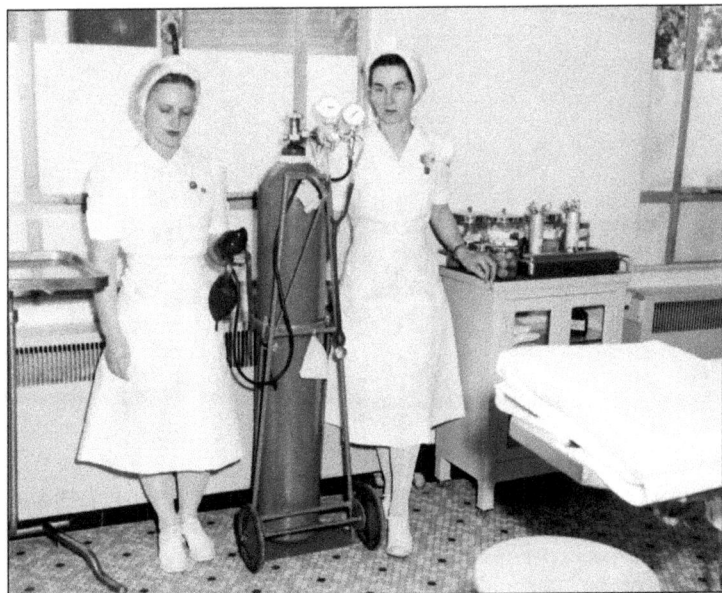

In the 1940s, McMinnville General Hospital was expanded to accommodate 50 beds, 20 nurses, and 3 doctors. Shown here, two nurses stand by an oxygen tank in the newly expanded surgery suite. An open house held on June 19, 1947, marked the expansion completion. (NR.)

During the 1940s, many communities around the nation, including McMinnville, conducted X-ray screenings for tuberculosis. An eight-county effort was launched that promised "No waiting . . . No undressing . . . No Charge." The aim of the program was to screen everyone over age 15. (NR.)

A fleet of six mobile X-ray trucks stands at the ready in this *Telephone-Register* photograph from the 1940s. "Free Chest X-Ray here" is displayed prominently on the sides. The United States and many countries around the world employed mobile units to detect tuberculosis. By 1961, one quarter of the US population had received a chest X-ray. (NR.)

Eight

SCHOOLS AND CHURCHES

William T. Newby understood from the very beginning that, to build a town, a school was imperative. Since it was "fashionable" for a community to feature a college, he donated five acres of land for this purpose. Dr. James McBride, William Dawson, and Sebastian Cabot Adams Jr. joined Newby in searching for the best spot. The others walked east, favoring high ground, but Newby judged on the side of practicality, "If the town never amounts to anything, the five acres out yonder would almost spoil my future wheat field." So, they walked south instead, on Newby's suggestion, and that is how the site of the future Linfield College was selected. Until 1877, younger students also received instruction at the college. Cook School opened its doors in McMinnville that year, followed by Columbus School in 1892, and the city's first high school opened in 1910.

The first church in McMinnville appears to have been the Christian church that was established in 1847. In 1858, Rev. George C. Chandler, a Baptist, organized the first Sunday school and called for the first ever prayer meeting held in the community. The McMinnville United Methodist Church was founded in 1854 and, about 1870, the congregation built a church on the corner of Second and Evans Streets.

Presbyterian residents first worshipped in a barn owned by Jesse C. Henderson, located on the Henderson Donation Land Claim on Donaly Road near Hill Road northwest of McMinnville. The group began meeting in 1851, with another congregation meeting south of town. In 1859, a union meetinghouse was constructed on the present site of the church (390 NE Second Street). That building was moved when the church traded it for a pulpit.

A Catholic church appeared in 1875 on land donated by William T. Newby. The original building stood beside the Buchanan-Cellers feed supply and was moved across the railroad tracks. Since the church was just east of the settled area of town, a wood sidewalk extended all the way to the parish entrance.

Cook School became McMinnville's first public school in 1877. Before that, schoolchildren were taught in the original L-shaped building that became McMinnville (Linfield) College. The building pictured was constructed in 1888. (CO.)

The 1927 second-grade class at Cook School poses on the front steps with teacher Ruth Messinger. The original building had six rooms, a large basement used for storage, and a playroom. Other early teachers included Anna Bean, Thomas Story, and Mary Hayes. (UL.)

Columbus School was the second public school building built by District 40. Constructed in 1892 across Cozine Creek from Linfield, Columbus School held elementary classes on the first floor and a two-year high school on the second floor. Superintendent Baker's 1891 report states, "A good house . . . can be built for $2,500." (CO.)

This photograph features the 1905 elementary class at Columbus School. There are 23 students and a teacher. Drawings on the blackboard include a house, an apple, and a potato; the Memory Gem reads, "Hearts, like doors, will open with ease to very very little keys; And don't forget that two are these, I thank you sir, and If you please." (DA.)

In 1910, the McMinnville School District built a four-year high school on the north edge of town, at Twelfth and Baker Streets. It served McMinnville high school students until 1957, when a new high school was built. Eventually, this building was demolished. (NR.)

In 1927, twelve students from McMinnville High School formed the Song Girls. Miss Clock (second row, far right) was their teacher. The girls would "install some pep into the student body," according to the yearbook. They also traveled to the college and different luncheon clubs to sell tickets, sing, and arouse pep. (CI.)

The McMinnville High School Class of 1967 planned quite an event for homecoming. Don Christensen is the student kneeling on top of what would become a major bonfire. The wood came from a barn razed on Don's family farm. Usually, an outhouse was placed at the top of the large pile of wood used in such bonfires. (CI.)

It was not long before McMinnville High School was overcrowded, as were the elementary schools, so the district built a junior high school. It was the first in the state and held classes for the seventh, eighth, and ninth grades. The original junior high building was later demolished, and a new structure was built. (NR.)

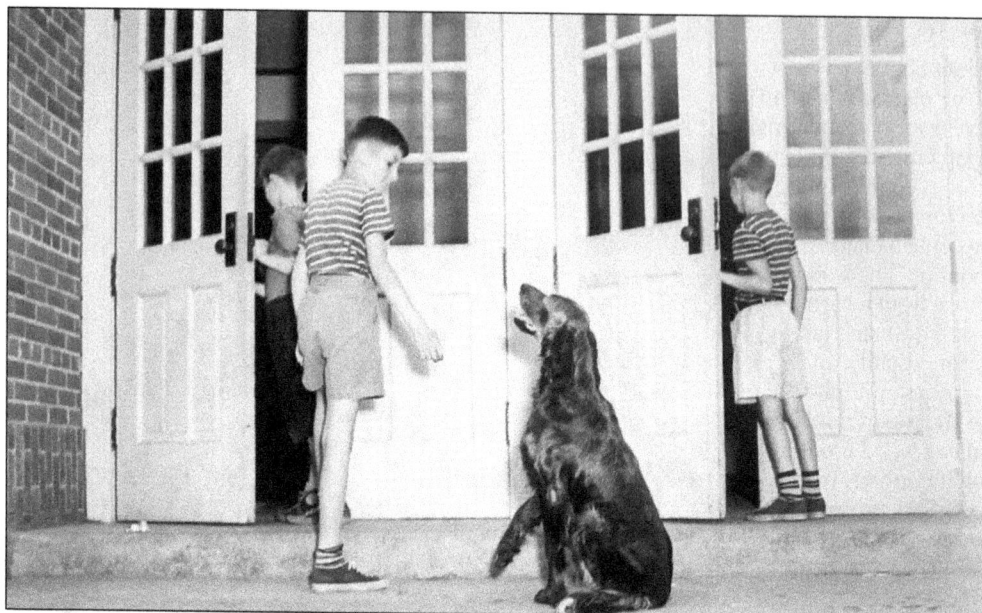

For the school board of McMinnville District 40, the week of September 6, 1938, was an occasion to celebrate. Voters approved $50,000 in bonds to remodel the inadequate and unsafe high school and junior high school buildings. The lad in this picture is not as happy, bidding farewell to his faithful friend to attend school that following Monday. (NR.)

The original Catholic school in McMinnville was built in 1906. The front door faced down Third Street. The building comprised a basement playroom, two floors for classrooms, and an attic. When it opened, only 40 children attended; by 1914, enrollment had grown to 90 pupils. In 1949, the school had 149 students. Some met in the gym while a new school was constructed. (CO.)

Catholic worship began in McMinnville when John Sax purchased the William T. Newby mill. Newby provided two blocks of land, and St. James Church was erected there in 1875. The structure was 24 by 50 feet and provided plenty of space for sheds, where horses were left during Mass. The original building was built across the tracks from the site of the church's future location. (Courtesy of St. James Parish.)

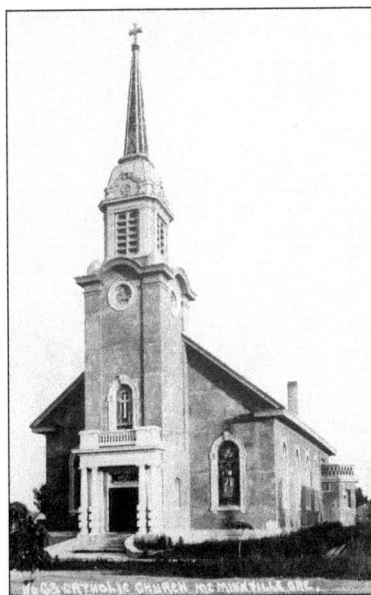

The McMinnville Christian Church was founded in 1847, before the town's formation. Area residents wanted to send their children to school and asked Aaron Payne, the church's minister, to provide instruction. Anyone from 6 to 60 could attend school for $5 per student. The year of construction, displayed above the doorway, was 1858. (CI.)

On May 11, 1867, a total of 22 members of the South Yamhill Church resigned to form a new body. Under the direction of Rev. J.W. Osborne Sr., they met first at the Cumberland Presbyterian Church. After petitioning to join the Central Baptist Convention, the church grew to 88 members by December 2, 1883, when members met in this building for the first time. (Courtesy of First Baptist Church of McMinnville.)

The First Baptist Church of McMinnville was founded by 11 men, 9 women, and 2 children. Cleveland C. Riley was the first pastor, followed by John W. Osborne Sr. and Wilson D. Meadows. Although the date of this photograph is unknown, it is likely early in the church's history. (Courtesy of First Baptist Church of McMinnville.)

From 1858 to around 1868, the First Baptist Church held Sunday school in the L-shaped building of McMinnville College, under Rev. George C. Chandler, the college's first president. The church's original building was occupied from 1867 to 1893. A second building was added in 1898, and the structure pictured here was constructed in 1926. This photograph, taken September 1, 1938, was for the church bulletin. (NR.)

The McCabe Chapel of the United Methodist church was built in 1886 by the Nelson Cone family, which consisted of six adult children and their families. The church, west of McMinnville, was named for Charles Cardwell McCabe, a Civil War veteran. The chapel did not have electricity until 1951 and still does not have indoor plumbing. Descendants of the Cone family still attend services at the church. (UL.)

The first building for McMinnville's First Presbyterian Church was constructed in 1859. In 1887, a second building was erected but burned to the ground in 1896. Only three items were rescued from the fire, the origin of which was unknown: a pulpit, the bell in the tower, and the pulpit Bible. The third building was completed in 1898 and is shown here. Note the gunsmith and furniture shop sign, which sports a rifle and a bedpost. (Courtesy of First Presbyterian Church.)

The 1904 to 1917 Presbyterian congregational choir poses for a photograph. Shown from left to right are (first row) Nora "Dolly" Jacobs, Maud Graves, and Sadie Gortner; (second row) Minnie Schenck, Molly Patty Warren, Frank Rogers, and Mattie Fender; (third row) William T. Macy, Genevieve Frisbie, Hervey M. Hoskins, Hattie Campbell, and Carrie Sherwood. In the upper left corner is Matthias U. Gortner, director; at lower right is Mattie Cureton, organist. (Courtesy of First Presbyterian Church.)

Construction on the current Presbyterian church building started in October 1909, with a dedication of the cornerstone. Several historic items were placed in that stone. Since then, there have been three major building projects, including the addition of an education wing in 1964, a 1993 retrofit for earthquake code, and a 2008 extensive renovation. (Courtesy of First Presbyterian Church.)

McMinnville Full Gospel Church was completed in March 1938. A dedication service was held on Sunday, March 6, 1938. The church was located at Third and Johnson Streets. In honor of the new church, evangelist Genevieve Booth-Clibborn and her daughter, Catherine Booth-Clibborn, held services with titles such as "My Mother's Prayers in Flames of Fire" and "When I Saw Christ." (CI.)

BIBLIOGRAPHY

Cawley, Martinus. *St. James Parish.* McMinnville, OR: St. James Parish, 1977.

Culp, Edwin D. *Stations West, the Story of Oregon Railways.* Caldwell, ID: Caxton, 1972.

Dirks-Edmunds, Jane Clark. *Roots, Vision, and Mission: The 125-Year History of First Baptist Church McMinnville, Oregon.* McMinnville: 1993.

The Eugene Register Guard (Eugene, OR), various.

First Presbyterian Church. *The Somewhat Incomplete History of Our Church Buildings.* McMinnville, OR: First Presbyterian Church.

Gaston, Joseph. *The Centennial History of Oregon, 1811–1912.* Chicago: S.J. Clarke, 1912.

Henberg, Marvin. *Inspired Pragmatism: An Illustrated History of Linfield College.* Portland, OR: Carpe Diem, 2007.

Holmes, Kenneth L. *Linfield's Hundred Years: A Centennial History of Linfield College, McMinnville, Oregon.* Portland: Binfords & Mort, 1956.

Huit, Katherine L. *History of Water and Light.* McMinnville, OR: Reflections Historical Research, 1988.

Jonasson, Jonas A. *One Hundred Years of Service, A History of the First Baptist Church at McMinnville, Oregon 1867–1967.* Self-published, 1967.

Lockett, Jim. *Pioneer History of McMinnville & Lafayette.* McMinnville, OR: School District 40, 1987.

Macy, Ralph William. *Wooden Sidewalks: Growing Up in Western Oregon.* Portland: Hapi, 1983.

Mattoon, C.H. *Baptist Annals of Oregon 1844 to 1900.* McMinnville, OR: Telephone-Register, 1905.

McMinnville First Hundred Years. McMinnville: Provisional League of Women Voters of McMinnville, OR: 1957.

News-Register (McMinnville), various.

New York Times, various.

The Oregonian, various.

Portrait and Biographical Record of the Willamette Valley. Chicago: Chapman, 1903.

Richardson, Brian. *An Extensive Analysis of the Business and Economic Climate of McMinnville, Oregon from 1885–1910.* McMinnville: Yamhill County Historical Society, 2010.

Stoller, Ruth. *Schools of Old Yamhill.* Lafayette, OR: Yamhill County Historical Society, 1982.

Telephone-Register (McMinnville), various.

The West Side, the Journal of the Yamhill County Historical Society, various.

DISCOVER THE HISTORY OF NEARBY OREGON CITIES

Images of America: *Salem*
Images of America: *Newberg*

coauthored by Tom Fuller and Christy Van Heukelem

Visit us at
arcadiapublishing.com

www.ingramcontent.com/pod-product-compliance
Lightning Source LLC
Chambersburg PA
CBHW050655110426
42813CB00007B/2015